Lovers—
WHATEVER HAPPENED TO EDEN?

OTHER BOOKS BY DONALD M. JOY

Bonding: Relationships in the Image of God
Re-Bonding: Preventing and Restoring Damaged Relationships
Meaningful Learning in the Church
Moral Development Foundations

Lovers–

WHATEVER HAPPENED TO EDEN?

Donald M. & Robbie B. Joy

WORD BOOKS
PUBLISHER
WACO, TEXAS

A DIVISION OF
WORD, INCORPORATED

LOVERS—WHATEVER HAPPENED TO EDEN?

Library of Congress Cataloging-in-Publication Data

Joy, Donald M. (Donald Marvin), 1928–
  Lovers—whatever happened to Eden?

  Bibliography: p.
  Includes index.
  1. Marriage—Religious aspects—Christianity.
2. Joy, Donald M. (Donald Marvin), 1928– .
3. Joy, Robbie, 1929– . I. Joy, Robbie,
1929– . II. Title.
BV835.J69 1987   261.8'35872   86–28090
ISBN 0–8499–0541–9

7898BKC987654321
Printed in the United States of America

To
Jim and Shirley Dobson
Co-Regents at Home
Joint-Tenants of America's Families
Joint Heirs of God's Grace

But especially dedicated to the veterans of our
"four seasons" adventures
with whom we shared the
child-rearing years
and now share the rewards of communal grandparenting!

Don and Elda Rose Bowen
Bill and Joyce Brenneman
Bill and Loraine Engleberth
Floyd and Dorothy Hollar
Del and Alice Keener
Phil and Marianne Smith
Rex and Lorabel Wildman

and whose marriages are exemplars of mutuality and celebration!

Please do not read this book without first discussing its content and tenor with Carlos or Carl.

Thank you.

△

vii

Foreword

△

"Preventive Medicine" for Your Marriage

It has been fifteen years since we began to make marriage
and family ministry a top priority. The decision began to
form one morning—around two hours past midnight, to be
exact. Returning from a lengthy house call on an emergency
run to help deal with a marital crisis, I tiptoed into the bedroom with shoes in hand. Helen whispered sleepily:

"It's okay, honey. I'm awake. How'd it go?"

"Terribly. They're not going to make it. There's got to be
a better way than this."

We began talking about the excessive time and energy we
had been spending in "emergency surgery" and decided
we would start majoring more on the "preventive medicine"
aspect of marriage. The decisions we made that night began
a search for premarital and marital programs which would
lay foundations to intercept trouble while it was in earlier
stages. We invested months in special training and in our
involvement in Marriage Enrichment and Engaged Discovery weekends. We have been joyously rewarded as we have
led hundreds of engaged and married couples through these

intensive experiences. We consider this one of the most important aspects of our ministry.

However, we soon realized that some of the greatest obstacles to marriage enrichment came from deeply ingrained ideas of husband-wife identity roles. These obstacles, ironically, turned up particularly among couples with long-term Christian backgrounds.

We found, as we began examining the patterns, that many problems, including those of communication, sexual adjustment, responsibility, and even spiritual growth, stemmed from a false theology of God's design for masculinity and femininity. We discovered that concepts often described as "God's Family Plan," "Headship and Submission," and "Chain of Command" often resulted in the undoing of much of the enrichment which had come with dramatic weekend breakthroughs for the couples. When we turned to the literature and seminars available, we saw that the vast majority promoted corporate and even (can you imagine it?) military metaphors to describe the marriage relationships. Worse, these concepts were all wrapped in biblical language which glorified the consequences of human fallenness and categorized relational vices and sins as virtues!

On the other hand, we were saddened that many Christians, in desperation, had turned away from Scripture and were looking to humanistic extremes in order to have a respect-based foundation for their marital relationships. For a long time we have needed a truly in-depth study of what the Scriptures really teach about God's design for male-female relationships and the nature of Christian marriage. Don and Robbie Joy have supplied that need in *Lovers— Whatever Happened to Eden?*

Following Jesus' example, who when asked questions about marriage, always took his audiences back "to the beginning," the Joys take us back to Creation and give a careful and accurate picture of God's original intention. They show the tragic consequences of sin as it marred that design. But they do not in any way attempt to "baptize the Fall" by incorporating fallen human impulses into God's family plan. Instead, in a truly scholarly way, we are shown the full, broad scope of the New Testament picture of God's attempt to restore his original design in a marriage relationship based on the "head" and "body" metaphor of the "one person" metaphor of Christ and his Church.

There is frosting on the cake. *Lovers* . . . is more than an excellent exegetical study of the important biblical passages on marriage relationships. Woven through is the honest, intimate story of the very human struggle involved in Don and Robbie's marital and spiritual pilgrimage. We completely identified with their story, as we, too, have climbed that difficult mountain with the magnetic pull of the Fall restraining our ascent. So we commend this book to all lovers, young and old, who want to enjoy the pure, fresh air and the exciting view from the top.

DAVID AND HELEN SEAMANDS
Nicholasville, Kentucky

Acknowledgments

△

Always in Their Debt

Until now, writing at our house has been a "solo" task. There have now been seven books, but this is the first "duet." Robbie really conceptualized this book and announced its priority even before *Bonding: Relationships in the Image of God* was finished. Her insight exploded the hope for *Lovers* . . . after she heard me preach a sermon from John 13 which I called, modestly, "Jesus Has a Plan for Your Family."

"That has got to be your next book," she affirmed, as we drove home.

But *Re-Bonding: Preventing and Restoring Broken Relationships* got front-burner attention for reasons which are revealed in its "acknowledgments." Still, Robbie said, "Jesus has a plan for your family" has got to come soon. And as usual, she was right. So we envisioned a plan: We would dialogue the book's format and content together. Robbie would actually dictate "her story" as a critically important part of the flow of the book. She was terrified of "writing." She keeps a journal and writes regularly in her vocation of teaching, but the thought of a keyboard and a formal manuscript was terrifying. So, *Lovers—Whatever Happened to Eden?* is our book. And it is the third in the "bonding series."

And we have agreed that our next project will include the abbreviated "bonding" project for which parents have begged us to give their teens. It will constitute the final chapter in the fourth bonding book, *Parenting: Launching Children in an Age of Promiscuity.* Interestingly enough, we originally designed a teen companion to *Bonding: Relationships in the Image of God,* but its photography format went out of control, and we didn't get beyond the first "format imaging" stage of its development. Now we will start over.

All of this commitment to the young has been accentuated in recent weeks as I have accepted a call to serve as a review consultant for the Office of Population Control in the United States Department of Health and Human Services. I have been asked to master Title XX, with an eye to evaluating grant proposals and offering critiques which might bring them up to the Title XX standards: Prevention of pregnancies through supporting of families and adolescents with educational programs designed to postpone sexual activity through abstinence. When the Secretary phoned she said simply, "I've been told that you have interest in such things and that you might be able to help us." I accepted on the spot.

"Turn Your Heart Toward Home"

Dr. James C. Dobson and his wife Shirley have been kind to us. Jim's scouts found us and aired some of our encouraging words on "A New Look at Childbirth" to a few million listeners on his well-established radio talk show, "Focus on the Family." All of us who sat through nearly four hours of filming at Cincinnati's Riverfront Coliseum in March of 1985, at the first "shoot" for "Turn Your Heart Toward Home," saw the harvest of what Jim had intimated to us during lunch when Shirley was ill. They not only live out a co-regency at home, by which either of them can "pinch hit" for the other, they also have a "joint-ministry" to America's families. Shirley's session at Riverfront was easily the hardest hitting one hour we have taken in recently. Shirley's authority was a full match for Jim's, and there was no competition, only the fullest kind of support for each other.

We do not mean to suggest that the Dobsons "have it made," and that they live out the Eden pattern without a hitch. But it is to affirm that no matter how they may try to interpret their relationship or define their roles, the actual image of their relationship, obvious to the two of us, is this: they are reflecting the doctrine of Creation. And we know from every other signal that their marriage and family are surrounded by the transforming and redeeming grace of Jesus. We offer a modest "thanks" to Jim and Shirley here, but the book is especially dedicated to them.

Enriching Our Marriage

You will read of the "pilgrimage of our marriage" throughout the book, but the final chapter will offer a blueprint based on where we have been. As we got "a new marriage" in the early seventies we were fortunate to be living under the shadow of the Wilmore United Methodist Church. Twice a year a special conference was offered: "Marriage Enrichment." John and Julie had spent the weekend in the program in about 1975. So a year later we put our names on the waiting list too.

Marriage Enrichment, in the United Methodist version based in Nashville, unlike some other similar programs, intentionally focuses the couples involved in making positive oral statements to each other. Husbands and wives spend a weekend being prompted, nudged, and coached into finding affirming things to say to each other. Then the spouse who receives the verbal affirmations responds at the "feeling" level. It was a grand, expanding experience for us. And our hosts for the entire event, the famous trainers themselves, were David and Helen Seamands. They gathered the entire group, after our extensive small group experiences, and in the church parlor gave us a "duet" on marriage—a full address, team taught. We echoed what another couple in our group reported during the process: "We wanted a better marriage, but as long as we focused on correcting what was wrong or weak in our relationship, it only got worse. But

Marriage Enrichment reminded us of this: we have a really good marriage that is going to become a great one because we will focus on the good and let the mediocre stuff fade away." We are in debt forever to David and Helen, and their guest foreword here indicates only a tiny fragment of the real respect which flows between us both personally and professionally.

As the Seasons Turn

Along with the "Salute" to the Dobsons on the dedication page, you will see another more intimate dedication. Alan Alda never met them or us, but our "four seasons" group does a Fall retreat together and a Spring "gathering," both at state parks between Wilmore and Winona Lake, the two holy cities which have been our bases since the late fifties. Now, for two summers we have added a summer "condo caper" for a week at Steamboat Springs or at Dillon, Colorado.

The nine couples of us discovered our friendships through the community of faith at Winona Lake, the headquarters of the Free Methodist Church where we invested a lot of time in each other's children in Sunday school, CYC, and FMY activities. We were so dizzy trying to help launch our families we were hardly aware that we were creating a set of relationships based on shared experiences which would see us through the rest of our lives—with eternity in view as well.

In those days we used to tremble and be anxious about whether we would see our children through high school and college. Now, we unpack slides and photographs and laugh and cry together as we enjoy keeping in touch with the unfolding sagas of the stories of our two dozen children, their spouses, and our grandchildren. This is our continuing "support and accountability group," and we rest comfortably in their care.

The "four seasons" conclaves are punctuated, too, by worship, celebration, and heavy theological reflection. "I was more comfortable before you told me that," Rex once said. But half a year later, he opened the whole theological issue again. And animal breeder that he is, Phil can consistently throw light on any biological or theological speculation I offer about fetal development.

But it is their marriages which Robbie and I have come to admire all the more as we see the unique balancing dynamics in each couple. We wonder whether it is simply God's grace that has so tuned and balanced their marriages. They are incapable of sarcasm, competition, or ridicule within their relationships. We wonder whether the ripening of our marriages well past the standard "mid life" median has something to do with the absolute commitment we see to our spouses. Bill Brenneman has turned "type specialist," using a modification of the Myers-Briggs personality inventory to let us discover our personality structures and to celebrate our strengths. That, too, may be a clue to the peaceable kingdom we observe within the couple units of our lifetime celebrants.

Professional Sounding Board

Living and working as we do in the shadow of a truly great freestanding theological seminary, the community of working scholars surrounds us. Yet the horror stories of "isolation" within the community of scholars are many. Here we have celebrated two "forums" within twelve months. In these sessions, faculty colleagues have marshalled their collegial energy to present, critique, and evaluate both previous bonding books. Coming to *Lovers* . . . we sought out the special critical readings of Eugene Carpenter, Old Testament linguist and specialist; of Fred Layman, our ranking biblical theologian; and of Stephen Seamands, our bright young specialist in systematics and theology.

You can imagine that no book written in an academic community would ever be published if it waited for a committee to agree on its content! So it would be wide of the mark if we were to suggest that Gene, Fred, and Steve would be willing to add their names to the authorship of *Lovers—Whatever Happened to Eden?* Steve has worked closely, co-sponsoring a spiritual formation group in weekly sessions for an entire academic year. And it was Steve, too, who put us into the "Trinity as intimate community" resources. He did it by saying one day, out of the blue, "I'm reading a book just now that reminds me of you." Gene has been a faithful prompter in carrying on an extensive oral and written dialogue about classical and linguistic clues to the "image of God" and the original "Adam" issues. And Fred has been able to furnish guidance in opening the literary sources we might never have found which deal with marriage, issues related to gender in Scripture, and to the history of interpretation on many more points of importance to our grasp of the ideas which undergird the main lines in *Lovers* . . . .

This disclaimer must be inserted: What is here is uniquely ours. Neither colleagues nor other partners can bear any final responsibility for material which may offend in any way. But to the extent that the book flows smoothly and the conceptual interpretation is helpful, these professional colleagues surely are our partners. In every case, the copy has been modified and enriched because of their contribution and dialogue carried on in the Asbury Theological Seminary community here, as well as among the hundreds of partners in the faith who have shared in our seminars on two continents.

Finally, in a salute which will go on for a lifetime, we thank Dorian, our daughter through marriage and through life quest, and John, our son. They have brought a reading no one else could give. John is a psychiatric social worker and lives in the world of addictions, marital crises, and the host of personal and social tragedies which surround the addiction rehabilitation services he provides through Charter Ridge Hospital. Quite apart from his pastoral and psychiatric training, John is instinctually a theologian. He is a competent and insightful Bible teacher, and his up-to-date contact with the popular and debilitating culture provides a net of censorship which catches double meanings and works the whole document toward clarity.

Dorian gave the manuscript the requested "onceover" and identified passages which "made no sense" except to the theologically trained. She remains not only our best link to the majority of people who urgently yearn for words of healing and hope, she also continues to endear herself to us by maturing into a stately wife and mother whose gifts of grace continue to come alive. And her pilgrimage is moving on. Recently she reported: "Mike and I came home from church Sunday morning and made a list of the things we have got to do this week. We were really hit hard by the pastor's sermon about looking for hurting people around us."

The energy for writing and rewriting, and editing, revising, and recasting all flows easier because this "cloud of witnesses" shows us such enormous respect. We salute them all for taking time to read the manuscript, for writing extensive notes, and for talking a lot of hours about fine points in the project. We are always in their debt.

Introduction

△

The Seasons of a Marriage

Here is the story of our love and marriage. When our children had a sneak preview of the manuscript it evoked peals of surprise. "You never told us about those things!"

Obviously; it was true. But how do you find the justification for "telling your story" during the harried childrearing years? And for the ten years after launching the boys, while we were renewing our relationship as lovers, their young love was so absorbing that it never occurred to us to do the "remember when" routine for them. But now that they have preteen children around the house, John and Mike and Julie and Dorian see us clearly as "part of the team" of resource experts on love, marriage, even child-rearing.

This book will be telling our story—in detail previously known only to God, we suspect. But it will also be tracing the amazing blueprint for human relationships in general and for marriages in particular.

We have a thesis: we think there is a way back to mutual respect, co-regency, and joint-tenancy. What we yearned for and anticipated during the years of our dating soon slipped out of our grasp. We never found a way to articulate it, perhaps. Or our ideas of "love" and our ideas of "marital relationships" were actually contradictory. So we made fine lovers in anticipation of intimacy and marriage, but when we married we found that we moved from mutual-respect lovers to adversaries, normally friendly ones, locked in a martial marital structure. We think we see a lot of idyllic romances turn into quickly cooling marriages, and we believe we are on to the secret of how to "defuse" that trajectory and put it back on a lifelong, mutually supportive marriage.

We tell the story of the "seasons of our marriage," and how we actually have had three distinct phases in the marital years. For perhaps ten years or so, as you will see in our unfolding "autobiography of a marriage," we have been convinced that mutuality was the characteristic we most wanted in our marriage. We were quite sure it was the Creation ideal and what Jesus wanted. But it has been only in these recent years we have discovered it is what Holy Scripture teaches everywhere.

Until a year ago, we had bracketed three New Testament passages which, we concluded, seemed flatly to contradict the Eden and redemption images that were everywhere else. Then, suddenly, without any special searching on our part, all of them collapsed. We tell the story of the deeper imagery of those passages in the book. What amazes us is that in our early life those three texts (which seemed to teach a very "vertical marriage" model) had thrown the entire Creation and redemption panorama into eclipse. We had built our "theology" of marriage on a three-legged platform high above the surging sea of God's pervasive picture of human relationships and of marriages.

One of our friends told recently how as a boy he learned the only safe way to look at an eclipse of the sun. A neighbor told him not to look at the sun directly because it would burn the retina of his eye, perhaps doing permanent harm. Instead, the neighbor said, "Punch a tiny hole in a piece of cardboard, then hold a white sheet of paper below it a few inches, and the light coming through the hole during the eclipse will reproduce the image of the moon surrounded by the rim of sunlight behind it."

"It worked," he said. "But years later, when I was teaching in college, I opened the subject with the science professor. He told me I didn't need a tiny hole in a piece of cardboard to see an eclipse. 'Just get under any tree,' he said, 'where the light is breaking through the leaves. Look at the ground and watch the shadows. Every one of the shafts of light will show you an image of the eclipse.' And I did it. It worked!"

Exactly. It seems to us that everywhere we look, we see the image of Eden imaged, produced, and reproduced. We read it on the faces of every bride and groom. We see it in the mellowing of the Golden Anniversary crowd. But we also see it in statements of Scripture which are descriptive, normative, and doctrinal. The images are everywhere. Thanks for celebrating with us.

DONALD AND ROBBIE JOY

Lovers—
WHATEVER HAPPENED TO EDEN?

1

Young Love: Can This Be Eden?

△

The sun shone brightly, unrelentingly. It was Dallas, Texas, July 15, 1948. I had executed my role as partner and son in the farming and wheat harvesting routine in Meade and Gray Counties in Kansas. I drove to McPherson to pick up Roger Boys, my best man, and Pat, his fiancee. We drove to Dallas at night to get a break from the summer heat in those pre-air conditioning days. Today Robbie Bowles of Dallas would become my wife.

I was nineteen; she was eighteen. A deep sense of responsibility overwhelmed me on the evening before our wedding. I had driven to the south shore of White Rock Lake. Roger and Pat snuggled close to each other behind us as the four of us took in the remarkable lake view. But Robbie and I leaned against opposite doors in the front seat, and I wondered whether I was prepared to take full responsibility for school bills, getting into my vocation, finding our housing, taking out adequate insurance, and getting ready to have children if that came with the territory. It seemed suddenly to be more awesome than I had thought.

Of course we were too young. We were not ready for the responsibilities. But then, we wouldn't have been ready at twenty-five or thirty either, and there would have been more complications to our separate adult lives if we had waited. And even with the White Rock reflective date, we never discussed the possibility that we were marrying too soon. We never thought of postponing, then or earlier. The time was right, and we were blessed to have families to underwrite our young love.

Beacon Church was new, but would not be air conditioned for another few weeks. Robbie's family had brought on a florist to decorate and to furnish a pair of impressive candlestands and to distribute several dozens of long white tapers tastefully around the church.

Three of us emerged from the right front wing: Robbie's pastor, my best man Roger, and I. I sang "I Love You Truly," and John Bowles, giant in every way, ambled down the sloped aisle with the loveliest woman in the land clinging to his arm. We have pictures to support my undisputed objectivity on the matter.

We were married. It was perhaps 110 degrees in the sanctuary. When we returned for photographs, after guests had greeted us in a receiving line in the narthex, the lovely candles had given up in the heat, had bent to inverted "J" shapes and were flaming up wildly, sending torrents of wax onto the carpet.

So here is the "rest of the story." This is our book about marriage, love, and the structure of the relationship all of us yearn for in a marriage. It would be preposterous of "the bonding man" to tell the story alone, so you will find occasional marked sections which are clearly Robbie's words and perspective. And some will be identified as mine. But most of what is here is written in the perspective of "we."

We are beginning with our earliest contact for another reason. We need to put our early marriage clearly in the popular and traditional "mode." In this book we are asking you to reexamine Creation and to take hold of your dreams of Eden and the perfect relationship between a woman and a man. And to do so will mean we will have to collapse several traditional misunderstandings of the Creation and of the teachings of the New Testament, as well. You may decide that you cannot reconstruct your image of marriage, at least not now. And we want you to know that is OK.

It took us more than thirty years to awaken to the pagan nature of our image of marriage. With a little help we might have gone into marriage with a higher view of each other and of God's vision for a man and a woman, but a little "help" might have paralyzed and immobilized us. Many young adults today seem a little confused about roles and relationships. So we are comfortable with everybody working in their own time to reconstruct their vision of themselves and their relationships. Do what you need to do with it, but if it helps at all, here are our early stories. If all of this autobiographical material gets in the way of your progress, go to the next or to any other chapter.

Robbie's Vision and Dream

Not many little girls are as fortunate as I was. My parents settled into a house on Alaska Street in Dallas before I was born, but I had both sets of grandparents only thirty miles away at Rockwall. The Charles Bowles and Robert Smith farms stood across a country road from each other, and if I had a marked calendar from my birth to age sixteen, I think our family would have had Sunday dinner on the farm at least nine out of ten weeks consistently. Most often we were at the Smiths. The house was teeming with aunts and uncles. My mother, the eldest daughter in the Smith house, had almost literally brought up the younger ones, plus, she would tell you, two other households of Smith youngsters—her cousins. My dad, John Bowles, was the oldest son, middle of three children in his family, but the last to marry, having done his stint in World War I. He also carried a strong sense of duty to look after his parents. So the Bowles house was occupied only by my grandparents.

The Smith house contained the lively menagerie of teenagers and even pre-teen children. My Aunt "Sue" is only ten years my senior. I got a great deal of mothering from Sue and Aunt Flynn. But the boys painted even larger images in my young mind. They were full of fun, vitality, teasing, and most of all were excellent athletes. They were like older brothers to me, I suppose, but my idea of what a man is, what strength and energy they possess, was formed from my

Smith uncles: Archie, Sport, Jake, and Harry. Perhaps the most gifted of all of them had died of blood poisoning in pre-antibiotic days, just before I was born. His name was Harold, and even in the wake of the grief that his death left, the other brothers went on to impressive high school careers in athletics. My greatest moments came when one of them would be playing in a high school contest that made it to final competition hosted in the new Cotton Bowl in Dallas.

While the Bowles family were comfortable with a moderately religious lifestyle, the Smith household was almost reeking with highly motivated Christian conviction and action. I loved to sneak away to Grandma Bowles who would let me have straight black coffee if my parents weren't along. The best I could do with other grandparents was to get sips of well "milked down" coffee, saucer cooled, under the table where the adults were talking. But Grandmother Bowles would also let me play her Edison records, which my dad had triggered by buying his parents a famous home entertainment center: the Edison phonograph. And Grandma Bowles' records were not religious. They were fox trots, mostly, with lively lyrics about "red-hot mama," and "Charley-my-boy." There was even a greeting from Thomas Edison to the soldier boys at the end of World War I. Today, those records are in our home, having been sturdy enough to survive the tornado which blew the Bowles home away just months after the death of the final survivor.

Across the road, however, Grandma Smith's Edison was well stocked with religious records about "coming to the Garden alone," and about an "old rugged cross." And Grandma Smith had a radio that had lots of religious music on it. One of my younger cousins once confided in her mother that when Grandma died, she wanted the radio, "because we don't have a radio at our house that has such nice church songs on it." And Grandpa Smith, even down through his serious deteriorating years, always assembled the clan for prayers on their knees before any Sunday or holiday ended, and the cars cranked up to carry the married children back to Dallas, McKinney, or Grand Prairie.

I tell you these things to give you some idea about the shaping influences on my idea about what a man is and what marriage is about. But I was frustrated. In the place where I lived and moved, I was not seeing boys who were likely to grow up to be very much like those uncles, grandfathers, or like my own father.

Growing Up in Dallas

I have now taught school in Kansas, Texas, Indiana, and Kentucky, and have seen many children coming through elementary school. I conclude that I was a very healthy young girl, compared to the spectrum of children I have seen in my classrooms.

From the earliest days in school, on up through the end of my career in public schools at the age of fifteen, I moved freely, developed good friendships, and felt reasonably "secure." But I knew there were pressures on me to conform to a value system a little at odds with the Smith-Bowles community of which I was a part. So my five-day week was in tension with the Wednesday night and Sunday experience.

For one thing, church attendance took us all the way from Oak Cliff to the south of Dallas and sent us through downtown and to McKinney Street just north of the present concrete canyon of the heart of the city. It was a small church. I tended to develop best friendships with people just a year or two older than I was, and these consisted of two girls mainly. And when I was ready to think about social events and dating, the guys their age, also much admired by me, were off to World War II in the draft.

My "other world" consisted of experiences I had at Trinity Heights Elementary School, then Boude Storey Junior High just two hundred yards from my front door on Idaho Street. Finally, I matriculated at Adamson High School. While I found friendships in all of these settings, I was constrained by one major decision I had made: I would not date boys who were not Christians. And in my parochial mind that was narrowing the field to about one percent of the population. While I am embarrassed to reflect on my narrow provincial views in those days, I am also grateful for the protection that came as a by-product of that restrictive perspective. I dated perhaps a half dozen times before going off to college. Most of the time I would put off any boy who asked for a date by making some excuse. On one of the rare occasions when I did accept a date during junior high school at Boude Storey, my escort arrived driving the family car. I cannot imagine how fourteen-year-olds were legally driving, but then things in Texas have tended to be frontierish, and maybe it was the law in the 1940s.

At any rate, Bobby[1] came to the door at 2910 Idaho, escorted me to the car, then drove the two hundred yards to the school parking lot. In his nervous state he released me through the passenger door, locked the car, and looked back to see the keys dangling from the ignition. He panicked. He knew he had to get another set of keys from home, so he dropped me off at the school event. I spent the entire evening with my girl friends without dates, and Bobby arrived just as the program ended. With his second set of keys he opened my door, then drove me the two hundred yards back to my house, and walked me to the door.

"Oh, I see my folks left a light for me," I said, and slipped through the screendoor. I turned around and said, "Good night." And I was home free.

Bobby called me the next week and told me he had intended to kiss me goodnight. I have no idea what I said in response, but I remember thinking, *That's what you thought, Buster!*

So, at fifteen, I was off to college. It was a Free Methodist junior college in Kansas. My mother had gone there to school, as had most of the Smith clan. Here, I thought, are boys I can trust. So all of my bottled-up social frustration had been stored for the occasion. In the first week I dated the son of the Dean of Women, a future college president, and a future bishop. But I was unprepared for the unwritten law of the campus: monogamous dating! So it was with much reluctance that I succumbed to the practice and was regarded as "going steady" with the fourth guy to ask me out. He capitalized on the campus climate, but in my heart, I was not ready to consider entering anything that looked like an exclusive and lifelong relationship.

What I Wanted in a Man

It was clear that I was going to have the summer of my sixteenth year to reflect on my dating experience at Central and to revise my strategy. But I was also reviewing my "criteria." I was now beginning to be sure about some things I wanted in a husband:

1. *Spiritual leader.* I wanted a man who would take all of the initiatives about religious, spiritual, and Bible matters. I wanted a man who spoke openly about issues of faith and the Christian life. And I dreamed of having a man who would open the Bible in the family setting, read from it, and pray out loud. Though my own father had not come to vital Christian conversion until I was eight years old, and we had walked the aisle to be saved together, I had seen strong, religious leader-type males of all ages at the Smith family gatherings. And I was in a church in which such men spoke openly about faith and assumed both public and private religious leadership. I wanted that. And I thought of myself as "not a leader," passive, not wanting to feel obligated to speak publicly of faith, or to take the initiative in opening the Bible or to pray out loud in public, though perhaps occasionally in some minor way at home. My own father, once publicly converted, assumed the spiritual leadership at home, largely enabled by my more assertive mother who "knew her role" and turned it all over to him and "wrote the book" on how to do the Smith sort of male-dominant spiritual headship.

2. *Decision-maker.* Free as a lark, making decisions all over the place and enjoying it, I still knew I was looking for a man who would say what, when, and where, and simply tell me that was the way it would be. My "dream" was of a man who would take all of the responsibility for making decisions and leave me free from having to plan, carry out, or pay for consequences of the planning. I wanted to be the wife, the nonparticipating stockholder in a marriage, secure knowing that my omniscient, omnipotent lover and husband would care for me.

3. *Goal-oriented.* I wanted a man who was going somewhere. I had no idea where I was going, or indeed whether I was supposed to be making any decisions or choices about my

future. No doubt this criterion in my list of things to look for in a husband is a simple by-product of the total passive, dependent woman I was creating in my model, by which he was to be the spiritual leader, and the decision-maker. If he did all of that, of course, I would merely be an accessory, an object he would select in some magnificent, omniscient way, and I would never need to assume that I was responsible for any gifts or talents God might have given me. It would be enough if God would call the man. I would become his "wife," an object useful to his calling and career.

4. *Sincerity and integrity.* I wanted a man who was honest and good and who had no previous sexual experience. In spite of the excuses I had fabricated to avoid dating the "pagan" boys at Adamson High School in Dallas, I was basically an honest girl. And I felt that God surely owed it to me to give me the reward of bringing an honest boy into my life. I was a virgin, and you could not have enticed me to date a boy I even suspected had slept with a girl.

Enter Don

I had been aware of Don all during my freshman year. But the rumor had it that he was "almost engaged." As it turned out, he was simply monogamous, and while he was evaluating a long-distance relationship in Colorado, he was not "dating around" on campus. When that terminated after his holiday visit there, and Don began to move in a sort of "group dating" cluster of pretty serious students who didn't conform to traditional "couple dating" very well and who didn't seem to care, I observed from a distance. Some of the girls in that group were good friends of mine.

I guess Don was respecting the campus monogamy, and so long as I was matched up with my number Four basketball star, he kept a discreet distance. I did break into his world, at the encouragement of some of the women in the cluster with which he moved. I asked him out for a Sadie Hawkins' date, on which I bought him a "tin roof" sundae.

When the basketball dropout began writing to me from the marines, I was not interested in continuing the relationship. I knew I was not ready at this time in my life for a commitment to anyone, so I did not answer his letters. I needed to be free to date when I returned to campus. When I had not so much as written him a postcard during May and June, he wrote to Don begging him to find out why I was not answering.

Don had a reputation for "being for the underdog" on campus, and guys in trouble tended to trust him with the truth. He still is the advocate of the poor and of those in trouble. In fact, when Don was elected student body president about the time number Four joined the marines, it was his commitment to the troubled and the poor which emerged as the real "platform" that got him elected, I think.

Don wrote to me during the summer and eventually visited me. Since he was out of the relationship he had been testing in Colorado, and since he now knew for certain that I would not be number Four's campus widow for either personal or patriotic reasons, I guess he asked me out for the opening Friday night of the Fall semester. He inquired by letter, of course. During the summer, we wrote occasionally, and he showed up on campus just hours before the Friday the 13th evening date was scheduled.

I saw Don once or twice during the afternoon. He was busy getting the details of the evening put together. It was an all-college reception, hosted by the Student Council, and of course he had a major role, along with other elected officers who worked hard with him all year. But not once did Don mention to me that he would pick me up at the agreed-upon hour: 7 P.M. at The Elms, my dormitory.

Now, you may see the contradiction in all of this that escaped me then. But I vowed that Mr. Joy would not find me waiting around for him at 7 o'clock, since he didn't bother to remind me of the date. No, sir. This is not a woman who will be passively waiting around like a wall flower. So I dressed in my best and newest clothes, and looking like a million dollars with a small tinge of arrogance at what I was doing, I determined to leave The Elms and go to the campus event alone a few minutes before seven o'clock.

I started down the two flights of hardwood stairs, alone, toward the first floor entrance, and to my utter horror, as I turned on the final landing, in walked Don. Our eyes met, and he gave me the most comfortable look. I know now that Don does not repeat or renegotiate what he has once promised. If he said seven o'clock there was nothing more to discuss. Whether he had made the deal two months earlier or only yesterday. Seven o'clock is seven o'clock. And Friday the thirteenth doesn't change. It was several years before I ever told Don of my brash impatience with the ambiguity I felt on that day. But from then till now, we have "gone steady." He never took me for granted by assuming that I would have an identical schedule to his.

And I was a little baffled, too, when Don insisted that I must continue in school, and that I should decide what brought me pleasure in learning and in life and "go for it." "After all," he said, "I am not rich nor are my parents. So I can't even buy the kind of insurance that would take care of you, especially if there were children, so let's look at your education as one form of our 'insurance.'"

I should have known then that my ideas of total dependency, total passivity, were under attack. But that was long ago, and neither Don nor I was aware of the likely changing shape of our relationship. I dropped out of school after that second year at Central. Both of us were awarded identical scholarships to Greenville College, but even so, my family felt the economic bite of limited resources. It was clear that if Don and I were to be married one year later, after his junior year at Greenville, I would have to work to pay for my side of the wedding. I resumed my education immediately after the marriage, and most of our lives we have continued to "leap frog" educational adventures as each of us earned degrees and certifications well beyond any reasonable prediction, given our social and economic roots.

Don's Dream: Marriage as My First Family Obligation

I think I had been looking for a wife since first grade. Perhaps longer. I was conceived in a family whose entire line up of siblings and ancestors, so far as I could see, had "coupled up." Early. My own parents had married when both were eighteen. Dad had completed high school in the Spring. Mother had followed a different course, and had spent a year with a married sister near my Grandpa Joy's homestead. She met my dad at church. It was enough to pull him to Indiana when she returned at the end of the summer harvest season. They were married in October.

Mother's brothers and sisters were all married before she was. Dad's older brother had not yet married, but was ready to. So the "number two" son married first, in his case. I came along soon enough to hold in memory the romances, the marriages, and the arrivals of the children of my dad's brothers and sisters. I am the oldest grandchild on the Joy side. Eventually there were twenty-one of us, and all but Eddie are preserved in a photograph taken just weeks before my grandpa's death and just two months before my own marriage—the first marriage in my generation of Joys. Eddie was born a week after Grandpa's funeral.

All of these details simply paint a bold picture: Marriage was adult work and opportunity. It was as much my responsibility to be getting ready for marriage as it was to be thinking about a vocation and economic independence. Marriage was a matter of faithfulness to the family: I would marry in full view of the family, sensitive to their values and traditions. My happy task was to find a woman to bring into the family structure who would be both attractive enough to win their applause and traditional enough to put them at ease with the "safety" of the Joy traditions.

Being Formed as a "Joy"

As I tell this story, I wonder whether this solid fabric of tribal tradition and expectation would have developed if my parents had lived in a suburban setting removed from the homestead. I was formed in profound ways by my Joy grandparents and by my dad's brothers and sisters. It is easy to imagine that they "imprinted me" by their early care. I was the "baby" and they were surrogate parents, both literally and figuratively. It was an enormously safe network of relationships. I was affirmed, disciplined, talked to, and evoked to speech and antics of all kinds by aunts, uncles, and grandparents who obviously treasured me.

And I was included in all "sex-appropriate" special gatherings. The farm work, the trips to grain elevators, the John Deere farm show meetings, the harvest-day daily rituals of skinny dipping in a gigantic concrete stock tank—all of these were "my world." In recent years, as I operate farm equipment adjacent to the standing ruins of that concrete water storage tank for animal drinking water, I am amazed that it stands only six feet tall. In memory, as I stand naked on the foot-wide circular rim I think it was a hundred feet across and a hundred feet deep. And it was full of the coldest, freshest, wind-pumped water on earth.

Sundays were special. In the country church carved out of a corner of a farm adjacent to my grandpa's farm, I found all of these relatives dressed in their best clothes. Over time, my Sunday school teachers included my Grandma Joy, my Aunt Ruth, and my Uncle George. I could tune in on adult classes being taught by other relatives and their peers—all godly people whom I greatly admired.

But on Sundays I was permitted to sit with Grandpa and Grandma Joy. During morning prayer we were on our knees. It was a convenient time for me to whisper to Grandma: "I smell gum." I doubt that I actually did, but she kept Wrigleys Doublemint or Spearmint in her purse, and God had to wink at our irreverence every Sunday while I got my chewing gum during the pastoral prayer.

Bringing Robbie Home

Robbie had entered college at fifteen, I at sixteen. There was a war going on, and some of us were cramming as much living as we could into our early years. I had even been admitted to the U.S. Navy's V-12 program, had tested out as a high school junior, and was on my way to getting a couple of years of college before I was of draft age. In one of the smallest high schools on earth, I had been impressed by the fact that Roscoe Marrs had turned eighteen in the winter of his senior year. Suddenly he said good-bye to all of us in men's glee club, and six weeks later he was dead in the Battle of the Bulge, and we were burying him in the Fowler cemetery.

So, when I heard of a program that could get me out of

fairly routine high school classes and into college and an accelerated program, Bruce Ramsay, my grade school principal, agreed to "proctor" the exams, and quite suddenly I, too, was snatched from high school. I was off to college to beat the calendar and the inevitable military duty at eighteen.

I had dated during high school. I was pretty tentative, however, largely because the family criteria were hard to satisfy. The one almost suitable woman was stolen away from me. She was married before her senior year. A year behind her in school, her "married year," I was also in my final year before shipping off to early college entrance. So, in the wake of that disappointment, I racked my mind for a suitable woman somewhere in memory. I found it in my fourth-grade girl friend. With considerable effort, I located her in Canon City, Colorado, and even visited her family during Christmas break in my freshman year of college. But it was clear that my memory was of a phantom girl very different from the now maturing woman. Still, I think, I was recovering from the grief of the lost relationship from my early high school years. I report the remembered impact of that first serious relationship in *Re-Bonding* . . . .

So after Christmas of my first college year, I "group dated," typically with a cluster of students, mostly academic types not caught up in the "dating whirl" of college. I became politically involved on campus and was elected student body president in the Spring.

Enter Robbie. I had met her during our first week of college—in registration line. There was brilliance, lightness, and easy conversation wherever she went. She had accepted dates with two men on the same evening during our first week on campus. Within weeks I was to learn that while she dated around easily, she slapped men who moved too fast to try to steal a kiss. That was interesting. When basketball season opened, the whole campus of men had backed off and "punted." She and the athlete with whom she had gone repeatedly public were "going steady," or so the campus word said. But, as it turned out, she had agreed to nothing like that.

When her athlete left school in April and joined the marines, we were all saddened, and Robbie was regarded with special concern. She now had a man in the marines, and loyalty to their friendship and his patriotism spread a layer of respect over the whole brief history of their dating.

It was her marine who wrote to me during the summer to ask whether I, the dormitory "brother" and newly ensconced campus president, would find out why Robbie was not answering his letters. Of course I would. I wrote to her late in June.

I inquired in person, in Dallas, Texas, on a Sunday during the Fourth of July holiday in 1946, a month before I turned eighteen. Our family was visiting relatives in Ft. Worth, and the relatives furnished the piloting necessary for a farm boy to find anything in a great city. Besides, they had a friend who had once dated Robbie and knew where she lived. He chauffeured us all: Clarence, Beth, Marvin, Marie, and I. I had already written to Robbie asking the tough question about her marine and her neglect of him. So, in a quiet conversation out of earshot of the families, I asked face to face.

"I am not ready for an exclusive relationship with anyone at this time," she told me, "but everyone on campus assumed we were going steady, so no one else would ask me out. We had some good times, but I sensed we were not right for each other and prayed a lot about it."

So, on Friday, September 13, 1946, the first major social event of the new college year, I called at The Elms for Robbie. We have been exclusively "going steady" ever since.

I knew at once that here was the magic woman. I liked her spunk, her vitality, and her contagious social grace and laughter. My introverted tendency to pull back from a crowd, to accept public responsibility only when "drafted" by more assertive people, was both intrigued and nourished by her.

More than that, she was beautiful, charming, and my tribal clan would recognize in her the exceptional and rare jewel who would enhance the family's future. So, by Spring break, it was time to "take her home." I already had a preliminary family endorsement. My Aunt Beth, sister to the college president's wife, had seen Robbie in Dallas with me, and had asked candidly, enroute back to Ft. Worth, "What's wrong with Robbie Bowles?"

It was a utilitarian question, perhaps, but Beth was an outsider who had been hunted down and captured for the Joy clan by my uncle. And I was not alone in thinking that Clarence had done a fine job in mate selection.

I went through the entire protocol to arrange the visit to my parents' home. Robbie's parents had to furnish written consent for the trip. This had to be filed with college residence hall authorities, and most important of all, Robbie had to be made ready for the visit. She had done her part. She had taken the bus to Wichita where her Aunt Sue lived. Together they had bought a new Easter outfit, appropriate to the maiden visit to the Joy homestead.

When Robbie showed the outfit to me I was elated at its beauty, but chagrined that she had violated a tribal taboo. The dainty hat was circled with a smart, but delicate ring of silk flowers. Robbie sensed something was wrong.

The Chauvinist Speaks

"My Grandpa will not like you in that hat," I tried lamely to explain.

It was an impossibly complicated problem. Grandpa Joy was consistently a delegate to the West Kansas Annual Conference. He was a "first generation" Christian in his family line, following my grandma's faithful religious commitment. But Grandpa became the "head spokesman" for religious belief and practice. My Sunday afternoons were enriched by the theological debates, interpretations, and stories told in the Joy homestead living room. Women cleared the kitchen, covered the leftovers from the noon meal saving them for supper just before evening service. But the men gathered in the living room, I on Grandpa's stool, huddled in ecstatic learning! There I had heard him occasionally enumerate what the membership covenant meant when in the ritual the new members promised to "forever lay aside all superfluous ornaments." That included buttons that buttoned nothing, all jewelry, including "finger rings of any kind," and artificial flowers, whether on the altar of the church or around the brim on a lovely hat. It also excluded the wearing of feathers, as being unnatural to humans, in however small a cluster, as in a man's hatband—"pure superfluous adornment." We were "simple life style people" before it was faddish to be that way. When Robbie and I were married in 1948, it was without rings. But by 1951, our denominational rules were re-centered in some principles which delivered us all from those austere marks of our spirituality.

As I contemplated our visit home, my anxiety lay in the conflict I felt. I wanted Robbie to "pass" Grandpa's inspection. I suspect he would have ignored the silk flowers, but I could not risk it. Robbie removed the ring of flowers, reducing the hat to the plainest headcovering you can imagine.

And she was fully accepted. In fact, as I squired Robbie around among the Joy clan on that Easter weekend in 1946, I virtually lost her to the attention of all of the significant male relatives. Grandpa seemed always to be wanting time to visit with her. My dad was in his rarest extroverted good humor. I, frankly, was glad to get back to campus where I could have a little time with Robbie myself. She had passed with flying colors. I had chosen well.

I am describing my view of my role and responsibility in choosing, winning, then shaping a suitable wife. It would be difficult for me to say whether I would have been motivated along the same lines if my tribal support system had not been so vividly present. But I am also describing these foundational concepts in order to report that they provided a strong basis for our marriage. Even though I was a few days short of twenty years old on our wedding day, and Robbie was not yet turned nineteen, we were highly compatible: her expectations of me and my assertion of my role with her matched at a surprisingly high degree.

I basically regarded my responsibility as follows:

1. Find the right woman.
2. Court her and win her heart.
3. Shape her into an acceptable person as defined by my own and my family's values and expectations.
4. Take full responsibility for her safety, support, and general well-being.
5. Control the environment, her vulnerabilities, and her lack of experience and competence by "being there first"

and by making decisions to guarantee her safety and to spare her having to choose, make a mistake, and be likely to be hurt.

In executing this set of responsibilities, I was fortunate to have gentle and consistent models in the uncles, grandfathers, great uncles, great grandfathers on all sides of my family. Not only so, but it was clear that they were doing what "heads of families" were obligated to do, according to the Bible. I listened at family prayers to the oft-repeated reading from Ephesians which tattooed in my mind the idea that "women submit to husbands," "children obey parents," and "husbands love wives." It all seemed satisfying. The roles and responsibilities were obvious to anyone. I was secure—not arrogant, I hope, but very secure.

But Who Was to Be the Head of Our House?

In all of this amazing, thoroughly Christian, and gentle clan there was an emerging paradox. In several of the tribal homes there was a poster framed or cast into plaster of Paris. I suspect that its message was both a statement of the profound mystery of many of those paterfamilias marriages in our extended families, and also a bold contradiction to the idea that men were obligated to be omnipotent, omniscient, and without flaw:

> "Christ is the head of this house
> The unseen guest
> at every meal,
> The silent listener to
> every conversation."

So any Joy male who might be tempted to rise up and claim "headship" of the marriage, the family, or the household, was served notice by the innocuous motto stamped in every conscience. This home has a Head; it is Jesus.

Enough. This is how the story begins. At nineteen, I would have declared that Robbie and I had indeed returned to Eden, had found the original love "as God meant it to be."

Today, nearly forty years later, it is clear to me that my

image of myself and of my wife was colored and distorted by
the Fall. I was a son of Adam. Robbie was a daughter of Eve.
As such we were living under a fallen vision of husband and
wife relationships. Eve had another name when they were so
spontaneously joined in "one flesh" as lovers in Eden. The
man called himself "Ish" and named her "Ishshah," or "my
other self."

In our highest moments we thought of each other as "the
other self," but our deformed image of marriage relationships set us up for the greatest vulnerability of all: regarding
ourselves as objects, not as persons. Perhaps that is the most
pervasive and indelible mark of the Fall. Men are seen as
"breadwinners," and women have been called "Eve"—baby
makers, the "mother of all living." But those roles were part
of the consequences of the fall; they were not God's idea nor
Creation's assignment.

This book is our effort to retrace our perceptual journey
and to offer an alternate perspective to any of you who may
be ready to join us in our pilgrimage of being transformed
day by day into the image of God disclosed in the Creation,
in Jesus, and in our continuing walk with the Creator.

QUESTIONS PEOPLE ASK

*Q: You surely aren't recommending, by your stories, that
teenagers should marry. Are you?*

A: We recommend to families, not teens alone, that together they decide some life priorities. Should you find that
"age" and "exclusive, lifelong bonding" come in conflict,
you will have little trouble respecting an early relationship
and closing your eyes on the age factor. Ideally, it would
be nice if our young were so consumed by school, aca-
demics, athletics, and vocational dreams that they didn't notice that they have adult sexual and intimacy needs. We have
supported early marriages for our sons, and we notice that
where all of the value issues are laid on top of the table,
families in high Christian commitment tend to choose earlier
marriage than the national average. And if those marriages
could be studied separate from all of the violent, even

"forced" marriages, the survival rate, we are quite sure, would be very high.

Q: Was there something different going on in your grow-ing-up years which made early marriage more feasible?

A: Perhaps. It was not hard to get a job either as a drop out or a graduate from college in the late forties. But our starting teaching salaries of $2,100 and $2,400 per year in Minneola, fresh out of college, do not sound like much financial security. Our impression is this: Times change, but man loving is pretty constant. Both then and now, the critical issue is whether the families are both emotionally and economically supportive of the top priority: the moral and emotional health of their young. When such a priority controls everything else, love always finds a way, even in runaway inflationary times, or, we imagine, in times of genuine social or political calamity. Nobody said life was going to be easy, affluent, and without sacrifice. Families fail their young, we think, when they put anything else ahead of their commitment to support the integrity of their young brides and grooms.

2

Co-Regency: "Let Them Have Dominion!"

△

"You can't do that to people!"

It was the bantering voice of my son. John is an ordained minister and a psychiatric social worker. He had just completed a first reading of *Bonding: Relationships in the Image of God*. And he was objecting to the concentrated theological assault of pages 15–18, in a chapter entitled "On Splitting the Adam!"

"What you do is ask your readers to abandon a view of Creation that they have held all their lives, and inside of four pages you assume that they will follow you and see it your way! But if they do that, they then have to reorganize everything they have ever thought about themselves and about all of their most important relationships—with parents, children, spouses!"

I smiled. "If you think it is shocking to them when they see it inside of four pages, you should see the look on their faces when I stand up on a Sunday morning, ask them to open their Bibles and show it to them in Genesis five, then chapters one and two." I had just returned from an extended tour in which I had been doing just that.

"But Dad," John said, "what you need is a whole book about that way of reading the Creation. It is magnificent and wonderful, and people will want to believe it. But you blow them out of the water and don't give them enough time to process it all."

"OK," I said, "I'll write that book, but it is one that your mother needs to take hold of with me. After all, it is the story of Man and Woman."

The Image of God

Only humanity is created "in the image of God." And whether one reads the fossil record or the Genesis report, the human is the latest arrival of all the living and moving creatures. We share the same "day of Creation," number six, with all of the animal kingdom. We are made of the same stuff as the animals: the dust of the earth. And they and we are given the "nephesh," or breath of life. But "image of God" consistently refers to the spirit and character "receptors" which are universally and unfailingly in humans, and not in any other part of Creation. God is Spirit, and we are created with a capacity for eternity and for valuing the self in greater measure than in material volume and weight. "Our spirit bears witness with God's Spirit," and only humans have a moral sense, grounded in the "image of God" roots of righteousness, holiness, and knowledge, as St. Paul observes in his writings. But there is more. God by "the image" is deputizing humans as caregivers and responsible tenants of the earth.

Jurgen Moltmann, in an insightful treatment of Creation, suggests that we are first of all *imago mundi*, "image of the earth," a finite creature which is "a microcosm in which all previous creatures are to be found again, a being that can only exist in community with other created beings and which can only understand itself in that community." It is not so much that humanity is above the remaining creation that denotes the *imago dei*, or image of God, but that humans are woven into the social fabric of the earth. An egocentric view of humanity places us at the exploitive peak of Creation. "But there is no mention at all in the creation accounts of enmity between human beings and beasts, or of a right to kill animals. Human beings are appointed as 'justices of the peace'" of the complex layers of the entire Creation. What is more, in this parallel role as *imago mundi* and *imago dei*, humans stand before God as the representatives of all other creatures. Adam "lives, speaks, and acts on their behalf. Understood as *imago mundi*, human beings are priestly creations and eucharistic beings. They intercede before God for the community of creation." Humanity thus stands "before God on behalf of creation, and before creation on behalf of God."[1] Such a view adds additional dimensions to the profound gift of the incarnation of God in the Adam, Jesus, who renews that investment in *imago mundi* by the renewed and more exact *imago dei* invested in Christ.

So *imago dei* denotes our place in creation as well as our spiritual potential. Does the "image of God" refer to our appearance, to our character, to our possibilities, to our attributes, to our function? Some of the above? None? All?

Let's rule out looks and appearance. If God sent Jesus in the "incarnation," it meant that Deity had to change form, shape, and appearance and enter into a form, shape, and appearance that was different from the existence as Second Person of Deity. When Jesus "became flesh and lived among us," it was an invasion by one order of Being into that of another level or order of beings—us. And we know that Adam and Jesus were two of whom it was said without any qualifiers: they are the image of God.[2]

The description of Jesus as being "the express image" of God gets translated also as "the exact representation of his being." So we are on to the trail of the essence of the image of God. We were made "representatives" of God on this planet. God so created humans that we mirror his own person. And if we eliminate the "look alike" idea from "image of God," perhaps "all of the above" then is the right answer.

We continue to collect research data on "moral development," and one of the absolutely baffling things about humans is that every generation is born with an innate sense not only of justice but also of attachment. These findings are nicely documented by the research and writing of Jean

Piaget, Lawrence Kohlberg, and Carol Gilligan in Europe and North America.[3] But humans are also innately endowed with a conserving tendency which we can only describe as "innocence." So if a child escapes abuse, there is an instinctual tendency to dream the dream of lifelong exclusive sexual intimacy. When that tendency gets measured by Robert Coles of Harvard, for example, he confesses his surprise that the children of the "flower children" of the sixties turn out to be quite conservative about their sexual aspirations and surprisingly restrained in their sexual behavior.

So-called "sexual liberation" is not inherited.[4] Innocence appears to be born fresh in every generation, and the sons and daughters of playboys tend to be gifted with the virginal, lifelong dream as they approach their first love. It becomes supremely clear that God has planted some of his character in humans. Perhaps the moral sense is the most distinctive aspect of the image of God. Any doctrine of "sin and the Fall" can easily document the human tendency toward evil, but that doctrine is incomplete unless it also accounts for the gift of innocence which we see in each wave of newborns God gives us.

We might think the "image of God" grants us "god-like" possibilities. And there is a sense in which we have been created "a little lower than God."[5] When you combine the spectrum of God's attributes with human possibilities, there are striking "shadows" of God's essence that leap out: God is omniscient, knowing past, present, and future, and humans hold the past in memory, the present in sensory perception, and the future in imagination. So a sense of history and destiny seems to be a uniquely human characteristic among the creatures. Other species seem to survive by instinct, almost "blind" instinct to take them back to breeding grounds and to repeat the life agenda that is virtually unchanged across all recorded history. God is omnipotent, and humans accept the charge to "have dominion" as a literal charge to tame the planet, if not the universe, asserting our ability to harness the wildest forces through our own insight and invention.

Whenever a composer, a poet, or a novelist creates a new world and populates it with sound, image, or plot, God's original creativity is somehow echoed again. It is no less

God's capital and gift that is being used when the music, the poetry, or the novel are obscene. God's "image" is a free and unrestricted gift. So when we drive to Bardstown to see *The Stephen Foster Story* most every summer, we revel in the beauty of the music but we come home in grief that such talent was so scarcely touched and so quickly wasted by an ironic combination of poor choices, bad company, and high dependency on destructive substances (which to this day are important to the economics of Bardstown and our own Commonwealth). A similar pathos appears in the popular *Amadeus* which chronicles the uncommon gifts of Wolfgang Amadeus Mozart combined with the almost analogous destructive force of political, ecclesiastical, and other demonic factors in his young and largely wasted life.

"Function?" Here we must put down our best thoughts on what is intrinsically human about humans. We cannot hold to a "functional" view of humans. If we did, we would be saying that people are valuable in direct relation to whether they are useful. A "functional" view reduces people to objects—things anyone may "use." And such reductionism is destructive because it "devalues" them.

We prefer to use the word "being" instead of "function." By "being" human, therefore, God must have had in mind that we would continuously and involuntarily "represent Deity" simply by being our spontaneous selves. So, when we teach parents about family structure and encourage them in their families, we consistently speak of "God's First Curriculum: Parents." And that curriculum is what all people are doing—teaching—every hour of every day.

Parents, simply by "being," are automatically "teaching." The best training for parenting, then, is teaching which enables them to be people of integrity, to make decisions hour by hour which are mature, and are free of deformed personal appetites and needs. In short, good parental decisions are made by parents who are safe and good people. We want every girl and boy to grow up to be mature women and men. If either should ever be regarded as "functional" bodies, it is at the cost of their true personhood. We can be sure they have been exploited if they are ever described in functional terms. You will notice that good people are open to learning from one another and participating in community. So parent development classes tend to attract parents who are open to improving the quality of their "being."

God has so invested his image in our humanity that it is inescapably in operation. We are spontaneously moral or immoral, but we are never amoral. We are helplessly caught, as by the "candid camera" photographer, in the very act of being ourselves. Fathers and mothers instinctively and spontaneously carry out a thousand operations in behalf of their children, and the "first curriculum" is at work. But so also do all the rest of us. We are pre-programmed to "be," to relate to other people, to comfort the grieving, to rescue the dying, and to reach out to touch the lonely and the sick. All of that is "image of God" representation. And if we choose to save ourselves, to withdraw from the impulses to help, to rescue, and to touch, then we are denying the image of God in us.

Genesis tells us it was this first human, this Adam, who was given "dominion," told to take charge of the planet. So Jesus told stories about a certain landowner who appointed a "steward" and gave him full responsibility for the land and left the scene. But the steward was accountable to the owner for faithful management. It was a story told to illustrate both the special role of humanity on this planet and the inescapable responsibility that comes with "being" the continuing "representative" of God. We are created "in God's image."

Bachelor or Complete Adam?

"So," you say, "what was John so excited about?" That is pretty standard theology. There is nothing new here. You could surely have said it all in four pages!

It is Adam who poses our problem. Was Adam a man—a male? Did God create a solitary bachelor in Eden? Or was Adam a complete, asexual, fully formed "image of God" solitary person?

Let's play out both interpretations. Both the biblical text and historic understanding and theology about Creation have offered both pictures. Living, as we do, in North America which gets its biblical theology from Europe and from television, we grew up, came to adulthood, took up vocations of teaching and pastoring, taught in the church, completed a tour of duty at our denominational headquarters, finally taking up residence in a graduate theological school community, all the while thinking, when it crossed our minds, something like this:

> God
> created a bachelor Adam,
> helped him to search the animal kingdom for a spouse.
> Finding none,
> God had second thoughts—afterthoughts,
> and generously created Eve,
> largely, perhaps exclusively, for the benefit of Adam.

Indeed, the word translated "adam" can go either toward "the earthling" or toward a proper name for a person. And in the first three chapters of Genesis, it sometimes seems to refer to the human species and sometimes to an individual person. Indeed, in some texts a peculiar marking of the word has been added later which indicates when it is intended to be a "name of a person." But in no manuscript or text is the woman named Eve until after the tragedy of sin. And there is surprising evidence that Adam was often the term that included the original woman.

Our first inkling from the text itself came from a footnote which the New International Version managed to print in microscopic type coded to the last word in Genesis 5:2: "at the time they were created, [God] blessed them and called them 'man.'" And "man" here, we are told in a footnote, simply is Hebrew "adam." "God blessed them, and called *them* Adam!" We hardly noticed that the "Community of Deity" had said in the opening chapter, "Let *us* . . . ," which certainly sets us up to discover humans created in community, plural, as well.

So "Adam" seems to describe a community which in Genesis five is described as "male and female." We looked again at the "image of God" statement in the first chapter:

God [who said "Let US make . . ."]
created [Adam] in his own image,
in the image of God he created [Adam];
male and female he created them.

And suddenly it was clear that this Adam may not have been a bachelor. Instead they were the Adamses! And the text was transparently clear following Genesis 1:27. It was "they" who were to "have dominion," to creatively manage this planet, and to fill the earth through their frugal and fruitful life together. "God saw all that he had made, and it was very good!" There we are. This combination of male and female, this "image of God" partnership was immediately charged with co-regency, with joint-tenancy of the earth. The text, in any translation, is clear. Peter, much later, would add the term "joint-heir" to cover the wife's relationship to the husband.

Now we had other questions: was the image "divided" between male and female? Or was the image planted in both the male and the female? Or in what ways did the "image of God" find expression in the humanity God created? The questions were larger, better, but even more baffling than we had faced before. It was about this time that we discovered a poster which described our dilemma:

We have not succeeded in
answering all your problems.
The answers we have found
only serve to raise
a whole set of new questions.
In some ways we feel we are
as confused as ever,
but we believe we are confused
on a higher level and
about more important things.[6]

Genesis told of the Creation a second way, this time in a narrative story with a central character named Adam moving across its stage. "The Lord God formed [Adam] from the dust of the ground and breathed into his nostrils the breath

of life, and [Adam] became a living being." Here we are
confronted with an account which poses problems if we assume that Adam is a bachelor. While we can identify with a
bachelor's loneliness in sexual frustration and need, or in his
despair that he will never, like the animals, be able to fulfill
his destiny of "filling the earth" through reproduction, it is
distinctly not sexual loneliness that is described. It is the
yearning for community, the hunger for a "court of peers" in
which to commune, and it is a polarized mutual dependency
that Adam craves. "It is not good that the Adam should be
alone" is the single reason for pairing the human creation.
So the materials invested uniquely in the image of God human are expanded into two persons, and sexual differentiation is first noted in Genesis two with that separation. The
story summarizes nicely:

> God placed a solitary Human in the Garden.
> God sensed that solitariness is no way to live.
> God ordered the moral environment: freedom and taboos.
> No suitable companionship was found for the Human.
> Surgery was performed to clone or to split the Human into two.
> The completed Creation delivered Adam: male and female.
> Both halves of the Adam magnetically re-attached.
> Together they form "one flesh."
> Their names are Ish (male) and Ishshah (female).
> They are not Adam and Eve. Not yet.
> They are Adam and Adam!
> Ish Adam and Ishshah Adam: the Adamses!

Today the traditional view, unanimous among European
and Western scholars, is that the original Adam was a bachelor. While some authorities urge absolute equality and mutuality for man and woman, based on Genesis one, they see
Genesis two as describing a "derived woman" whose role is
primarily that of functional servitude to Adam from which
she was drawn. You will even find some popular speakers
splitting hairs to tell you that "Adam, the bachelor male, was
given the image of God, but the woman does not bear the
image." Never mind, look at the Genesis text yourself.
Check one English translation against another until you can
decide for yourself what is going on.[7]

Yet the earliest Christian interpreters saw the Creation much differently. And it may be worth our taking a second look. We are impressed with the larger, more global and panoramic images of Creation and of God's work in history. And we have been baffled by tragic distortions implanted in marriages and in families by the Western version of Creation. But it was the mystery of fetal development, partly put in public focus by the tragedy of widespread abortions, that stopped us cold. Our mouths drop open at the mystery and wonder of human conception and of the re-creation that may provide a window on the original forming of the first human.

When we drop back to look at the images, metaphors, and millenial murals which emerge from Scripture, we see a magnificent pair of images. The two of them serve both to launch and to culminate inspired holy Scripture. There were *two named Adam*. Both are designated as unique bearers of the "image of God." From the beginning to the end of revealed Scripture they stand like sentinels pointing to God. In the beginning was what we have called the Alpha Adam. And at the closing crescendo of biblical time, God speaks again in his Omega Adam.[8]

God Created Them Male and Female and Called Them Adam

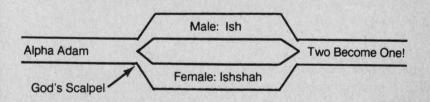

God Has Spoken in His Son. . . the Second Adam

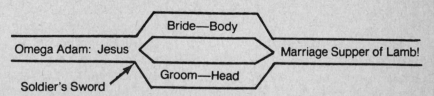

Among the ancients, in Jewish understanding, and among the early Christians before the "Caesarean captivity of the Western church," there was widespread acceptance that the original man and woman were formed from a solitary but whole Adam, as any reading of any translation of Genesis two would suggest.

Philo Judaeus, born about 20 B.C., was a first-century theologian. He may have been the first theologian to object to a view of a "complete Adam" containing all that is human. He argued against the then traditional rabbinic interpretation which held that Adam contained both sexes, insisting that the derivation of woman out of Adam was allegory, not history. But many of the church fathers took exception to Philo. He was unable to cite any rabbinic authority who did not take Genesis and the plural Adam seriously. Justin Martyr who lived from 100–165 A.D. and Tertullian who lived from 160–230 A.D. follow Philo's interpretation of the two accounts in Genesis, including the plural Adam, but both take it straightforwardly and seriously.

The interpretation continues across the centuries and is especially clear in the Jewish rabbinic tradition. Rashi, a famous rabbi (1040–1105), declares, "The Midrash explains that man as first created consisted of two halves, male and female, which were afterwards separated."[9] And Moses ben Maimon, known best to us as Maimonides (1135–1202), Spanish rabbi and scholar, supported an interpretation which saw the first human as a man-and-woman creature with two faces turned in opposite directions. During the Genesis two separation, Adam was put to sleep while the genuine feminine half was taken from Adam to make her a distinct and separate person.

Who can say why the Christian church began to read Genesis and Creation in a way to center attention on a bachelor male Adam? Was it the effect, as Jurgen Moltmann suggests,[10] of a monarchial Roman "takeover" of the Christian movement in a bold stroke of political genius which verticalized even our doctrine of the Trinity? In that takeover, was the family also made to conform to this vertical, pagan model? In the development of language did the "confusing generic masculine forms" follow political structure, thereby allowing a fallen cultural pattern to dictate thought? Or may it have been a mysterious shifting in reasoning processes by which the global, imaging, intuitive understanding of ancient humans was carried East while the analytical, hierarchical, managerial brain dominated in the West?[11]

And what do you make of the fact that a similar story line shows up in virtually all religious traditions from the Middle East?[12] We meet occasional scholars who are embarrassed at the similarities between ancient and pagan myths and the Judeo-Christian Scriptures. But why should there be any need for shame in acknowledging that there is a persistent "mythology" in pagan and non-Judeo-Christian traditions of a single "humankind" plural first human? The Judeo-Christian account is uniquely authoritative, uniquely and unself-consciously waiting to be discovered and matched with all other evidences. And Genesis stands alone among the Creation accounts in a significant way. Whereas the other traditions commonly invest deities with sexual and reproductive energy (and surround the human origin in fertility implications), the Genesis account offers us a virginal, idyllically high sanctity story of sexual innocence and purity, and keeps Deity nicely distanced from sexual innuendoes with the new creation.

As C. S. Lewis would say,[13] all of the other stories demonstrate how urgently the entire human race cries out to anchor its origin in some distant dignity. In the spirit of what he says about another issue, Lewis would suggest that the myths are evidence of a deep human yearning for a common history and destiny for men and women—a hunger for mutual respect and co-regency. What the Judeo-Christian Scriptures offer us is quite another kind of witness. They set down the record to indicate that it really did happen once. The Holy Scriptures through divine inspiration have preserved for us a record which is never out of date and which awaits every generation of scholars not only in theology but in biology, archeology, and paleontology. To illustrate, Lewis points out that the myths of resurrection pop up everywhere. Those myths are gesturing toward a reality which the people knew intuitively to be true, even necessary. But it happened only once—in the actual resurrection of Jesus.

Yet all cultures and all peoples hoped for it. So a certain uniformity between Genesis and the surrounding myths may say the same sort of thing: Man and woman are co-equal, co-originals, co-regents, joint heirs, and joint tenants. We hoped it always, and now that we have looked again at our Bibles, we have the text to support the dream all along. Even in English, if we had only Genesis two, the creation sequence is clear:

1. Adam.
2. Female and male formed from Adam.
3. Reunion in sexual bonding: one flesh.

So we see the most elegant picture imaginable: first a woman formed and fully self-conscious as a sexual being, then an awakening male, also self-conscious as a sexual person, and he is speaking:

> "This is now bone of my bones
>   and flesh of my flesh;
> She shall be called Ishshah,
>   for she was taken out of Ish."
> For this reason an Ish
>   will leave his father and mother
> And be united to his Ishshah,
>   and they will become one flesh.
> Ish and Ishshah were both naked,
>   and they felt no shame.
>
> Genesis 2:23–25

What we miss, given our traditional way of looking at the text, is precisely what might have prevented us from misusing the Creation to deform our marriages and other social structures: The woman and the man have an absolutely common origin. All of this is true whether you think of the original Adam as a male or as an undifferentiated "total human." The evocative reality which brought forth the first recorded human speech was precisely that the woman was uniquely "made of the same stuff," thus meriting an identity equal to the man's. He names her with a "relational" name which defines her value as identical to his own. She is not "different from him" in rank or order or identity. She is not, like the animals, "outside of him," but is one with him. We also miss the clear teaching which the ancient Jews saw at once: There is no mingling of human intimacy with the animal kingdom. Bestiality would never do. Humans are made for exclusive and intimate relationships only with humans: bone of bone, flesh of flesh, one flesh, naked and unashamed!

Image of God: Male and Female in Every Person?

Remember that the "image of God" is primarily and persistently a way of distinguishing the human creation as more intimately connected to the Creator. Remember, too, that the "image of God" denotes an off-print of God's spirit and of God's character, especially righteousness, holiness, and knowledge. But in this chapter we are eager to look at the concept that the image of God is carried through our male and female differentiation in some unique way. Our sexuality is the vehicle of our participation in the human race, and our sexual identity becomes the most deeply ingrained aspect of our sense of worth and of adequacy for remaining in the human community. "It's a boy!" or "It's a girl!" is the lifelong, re-echoing statement of identity for all of us.

You could conclude that we came to our "conversion" in the way we understand the generic nature of Adam simply by poring over the Genesis chapters. We were prepared in quite another way to go back to Creation to look at Adam with new questions. Looking back over the last ten years or so, we often speculate that if we had only mastered Hebrew in seminary, we might have seen the Adam problem earlier. But, given our tendency to embrace the familiar, we worry that we would have learned Hebrew with the same stereotypes that have guided most translators of most English Bible texts. Indeed, most commentators seem hopelessly bound up by the "bachelor pronouns" for Adam.

We shudder to think that we might have missed the catalytic moment. Had we learned in the company of respected mentors that the word commonly translated "adam" is also the generic word for "man," we might have been insulated against contemplating that we had inadvertently assigned gender through a generic English term. It was not the Bible text in any language that turned our heads back to Creation. It was biology. It was "Creation under the microscope of medical school" that sent us back to Genesis.

We have certain obligations to human development research—a field which we entered through the "back door." In research finished in 1961,[14] we uncovered a shocking sex difference in the ways boys and girls respond to basic religious education. The male-female difference was not one of degree. It was a difference in direction! Since those findings almost twenty years ago, we have been reading authors, both men and women, who have been on the trail of intrinsic sex differences. We have been consistently reporting the best and latest of our findings in our teaching and writing.

When all of the social and cultural differences are stripped away, it is clear that there is, at last, one unrelenting fact: males and females are biologically different. And the differences are more than the biology of genitals. It is nearly two decades now, since our discovery of the differences between boys' and girls' responses to religious instruction. None of us lives long enough to find answers to immediate questions, let alone living long enough to go on to formulating better questions. And as often as not, we are quite unaware of the importance of something the first time we see or hear it.

It was that way with the amazing truth about human fetal development. We first examined the story in a Jo Durden-Smith feature in *Quest/80*,[15] or a little earlier in Susan Muenchow's article in *Parents*.[16] But when, in a psychiatric handbook, we saw a citation to M. J. Sherfey's *The Nature and Evolution of Female Sexuality*, we tried to order a copy of the unpublished paper, only to find that a relatively recent paperback was available by the same title. M. J., you guessed it, was "Mary Jane." We were on our way to serious investigation of the biology of Adam!

We found ourselves reading in yet another form the new story of the planting and formation of the human fetus. The mother's "x" chromosome dictates the morphology or body shape of the early fetus, even though the father's chromosome selection may be "y" to sidetrack the mother's code. A boy is formed from an "x + y" combination. But the mother's dominant code still dictates a "female body" for the customizing job that yields a male baby. And both baby boys and full-grown men carry breasts as proof of the original morphology of Adam. As late as the ninth week, the clearly human fetus is distinctly female in form, complete with internal gonads which appear to be ovaries, and with an open vagina. Should anything interfere with the mother's relatively thin supply of androgens (male hormones), or should some ovarian cyst or other problem elevate her estrogen level (female hormones), that "xy" baby boy might be born with his original female-looking body. Boys are "made of" little girls, you might say. Indeed, Dr. Sherfey ventures that Genesis is wrong in giving us an "Eve out of Adam" story. A more plausible order, she asserts, would have been an "Adam out of Eve" story.

But Mary Jane Sherfey is likely wrong, just as our "bachelor Adam" ideas may have thrown us off into a pattern of devaluing women. Our infantile imagination had a heroic but incomplete bachelor in the original instance, with God providing the woman as a gift or bonus. Mary Jane can lead us down an equally violent interpretation: God creates a woman, and afterward turns part of her into a male. If we are both wrong—indulging as we most often do in our egocentric fantasies—then Genesis five and Genesis two may at last get our full attention: God is infinitely grander than anything we understand by "male" or "female" or by any combination of them: "God created them male and female and called them Adam."

If human sexuality in any sense represents God, it is as metaphor to Reality, and there is no literal correspondence which can attribute sexuality of any sort to God. Yet our sexual identities are the most useful and happy metaphor available to God who created both us and the universe. So God chooses our maleness and our femaleness and "consecrates" our sexuality to "image God" in the world. At the earliest moment, the embryo of male and female have a common form. We all start out the same in Adam, but we also all start out the same in embryo. Creation revisits every conception.[17]

And here we come to an amazing truth. Whoever this Adam is, the problem is not sexual or reproductive. It is loneliness. After the woman and the man are formed as sexual opposites, each male and each female carries in itself the presence and even the chemistry of the other. It is most obvious in the genital and reproductive systems, but it is also evident in the organization and modification of the brain.[18] But those traces of each other also appear in the very chemicals of the bodies. All males carry traces of estrogens. All females carry traces of androgens. Both systems actually produce the opposite hormones. And by mid-life, the mellowing of the personality seems to be matched by a toning down of the original hormonal production. It is common for armchair philosophers as well as Yale researchers to cite a trend in men toward "being more in touch with their feminine side," or in women "being more masculine in their independence and assertiveness" when observing the trends which appear with high regularity in the aging process.

I notice that I, Don, am gentler, more affectionate with my grandchildren than I was with our sons at comparable ages. It is I who have changed. It would be easy to say that I have been reading up on child-rearing and on sex differences and I have been delivered from my earlier stereotypes. Who can say? But it appears that my very physiology has paved the way for me to express more maternal feelings than I found myself doing spontaneously when I was twenty-five.

And I, Robbie, am more assertive, confident, and independent now than when I was a new bride and lover. Perhaps the complicated careers we have developed have made my autonomy essential, but I find enormous peace in each new epoch. I embrace the new experiences and new opportunities with a sense that I was created to "have dominion" and full authority in a wide sphere of responsibility. I have much more to offer in our marriage now than I could have ever thought possible. Our opportunities and our decisions are now really "con-jointly" made, and we make better ones than when I was helplessly dependent on Don to be the "decision-maker."

So we can read Genesis and say that the image of God,

male and female, is intrinsically written into every solitary son or daughter of Adam. If so, then marital status, age, and living arrangement are irrelevant to the central truth of what it is to be human: it is to be created in the image of God. There is no "missing half" in any ultimate and tragic sense. Whether a person might be a prisoner in blinded solitary confinement, or an anonymous pedestrian in a flea market in Madrid, the value of the person lies in the distinct gift of human personhood. It is as if God is saying both intimately and personally, "You are my image in the world" regardless of circumstance, location, or condition. "Be a witness to my dignity, my value, my character."

Image of God: In the "One Flesh" Union?

The original "one flesh" union of the man and the woman forms the dominant picture of the full spectrum "image of God." Differentiated, as they were, by the scalpel of God and formed into two distinctly and dominantly charged models—male and female—their first and almost involuntary response was to reach out and to re-attach to the missing other half.

It is here, no doubt, that Dietrich Bonhoeffer and Karl Barth properly shocked us into looking back into Genesis at the image of God.[19] We repent of our knee-jerk repudiation of the Bonhoeffer-Barth suggestion, not because of a theological conversion of any kind, but because of observations made in the education, nurture, and evangelism of people in families and churches. What we have observed now for nearly forty years in our caring vocations is something like this:

> God created polarized male and female with hormones charged!
> They instantly, perhaps symbiotically, "snapped back together."
> The polarization still motivates "pairing off" and marriage.
> The masculine-feminine polarization peaks from pubescence to 40.
> Parenting tends to occur during the decades of the polar years.

Children, therefore, tend to experience their models
polarized.
So, both biology and environment combine to "teach" sex
roles.

All of that works well and the results tend to be quite positive. But if either father or mother disappears out of the life
of a child, there are predictable deformities and often a lifetime to pay for the vacuum of a missing side of the "image of
God representative."[20]
So we might say that the spontaneous and highly reward-
ing and effective "image of God" witness in the world is the
paired marriage, where male and female combine intimately to form God's first curriculum to emblazon God's
character in the mind of every young child. But we must
also say that this elegant, almost regal and celebrative model
of the "image of God" is not its only or even its primary
form. The image of God is never more magnetically represented, perhaps, than in holy matrimony and the subsequent
intimacy of the family. But the image of God is vastly more
visible in the world than it would be if it showed up only in
the elegance of the male-female marital witness.

Image of God: In Community?

Since it was not good that the complete Adam should remain alone, even though created in the image of God, it
may be worth considering whether the image of God may
be primarily visible "in community." That is, "wherever two
or three of you gather" the image of God may mysteriously
appear.

We sometimes indulge in a mental game by asking, "If a
tree falls in the forest and no one is there to hear it, does it
make any noise?" We can answer the question on several levels: The sound vibration level, the auditory receptor level, or
the outside, impartial, even omniscient observer level. And
we get both yes and no answers.

Suppose we ask whether "the image of God" is present in
the privatistic world of solitary persons who withdraw from
social or communal contact. We likely could get both yes

and no answers again, when viewed from several levels: (1) what God has invested in individuals, (2) how the image of God is perceived or recognized, and (3) what the criteria are by which an objective observer might say whether, indeed, God had visited the place in the infallible image of his representation through human witnesses.

Self-esteem, while being housed internally and being monitored inside the self, is likely a gift which comes from "community." The feedback we get from significant other people signals us much like bids from the crowd as the auctioneer calls out the going price. We take seriously how others regard our worth. So parents who abuse, molest, or assault their children are giving feedback which devalues the child, and we can predict long-term damage to self-esteem. In contrast, we read our value in the faces of people who know the truth about us. If they can forgive us, we are forgiven; if they withhold forgiveness and instead heap shame on us, we sink into the depths of devalued self. We may even become suicidal as self-esteem drains out.

Watch the effects on you of coming together in "safe and holy community." Most often we sense the nearness of God when we are in substantial (not trivial and superficial) small groups. These are settings where people are able to say serious and honest things to each other.

"I don't know where else to say this," Steve announced yesterday at lunch, "but I need to tell somebody how proud I am of my wife. Angeline finished defending her Ph.D. dissertation last week, you know, and we were simply elated that everything went well. She has been given a grant to underwrite her participation in a conference on the family coming up this summer in Kansas City. I just needed to report that to somebody." Exactly. Wherever the "character of God" is present it is characterized by "rejoicing with those who rejoice" as well as "weeping with those who weep."

So here is a spectrum of possibilities about the Creation teaching on the image of God. Perhaps each of the possibilities is a part of the truth: The image of God in Adam is originally in a complete Adam. The image of God is also in every differentiated male and female. The image of God is exhibited in all "one flesh, naked and unashamed" celebrations.

And the image of God materializes in our midst when we come together in community. Jesus promised it: Where two or three are gathered in his name, there he is in their presence.

Rib, Side, Woman, and Bride

So "God created them male and female and called them Adam." The image of God is many splendored, is specific and individual, but is also general and communal.

What of the text which says that the Lord God caused a deep sleep to fall upon Adam, and while Adam slept, God took "one of the ribs" of Adam, and closed up the flesh at that place? Does this picture suggest anything about the relationship of the man to the woman when the surgery and anesthesia are past?

The word translated "rib" is nowhere else in the Old Testament translated that way. Indeed, its most frequent use seems to be related to construction, and in references dealing with the building of the Tabernacle the word is translated "beam," "chamber," "plank," "corner," "sidechamber," and "side."[21]

When the Hebrew Old Testament was translated into Greek, the Hebrew *tsela* in Genesis two became *pleura*. The Lidell and Scott *Lexicon of Classical Greek* offers several translations for *pleura*, noting that only in its plural form might it refer to a set of ribs, but its more common translation is to "side," "side of a man," even the membranes that line the thoracic cavity. They observe that the term may also refer to "wife," as the Hebrew *tsela* sometimes signifies a bosom friend, a person who is "at one's side."

If Adam's "rib" were formed into the woman, then we can imagine the original case of human cloning, in which a tiny microcosm of one person is built up into a fully formed second person. If, on the other hand, it is Adam's body cavity that is opened, we can also imagine a sorting and differentiating of male from female. The effect of either set of images is the same: male and female are from a solitary source: Adam. In any case, the appearance of Adam constitutes what C. S. Lewis calls "a miracle of the old Creation."

Even So, Come!

With the opening of Adam's side, another vision appears. St. Paul painted the original theological strokes by referring to Jesus as "the second Adam."[22]

Suddenly the horizontal Adam who, under the scalpel of God becomes both husband and wife, is replaced by the second Adam. This vertical Adam of ours hangs out there on a cross, and on the darkest of all possible days God turns away. And it is the tip of a Roman soldier's sword that opens the *pleura*. And the second Bride appears. She is, of course, the Church, our Mother, our primary, continuously caring spiritual Parent and the mode in which we experience Jesus—in the faith community.

So, history which began in a garden with the nuptial magnet bonding the original Adam—Ish and Ishshah, will come to its ultimate triumph as the Groom appears to his waiting Bride, dressed in white—Christ and the Church. And we will be there at the marriage supper of the Lamb. Christ the second Adam is also male and female.

In this chapter we have wanted to re-open the Creation of Adam and let you examine it for yourself to discover several major reconstructions that may be overdue. These transformations may yet give us a view of men and women which will bring us nearer to God's view of us. We have wanted you to look at some lines of historical interpretation and to ask any questions that come to mind when you look at the nature and possibilities of the original Adam, especially when we accept the grace of the last Adam to grasp the reality of our redemption.

QUESTIONS PEOPLE ASK

Q: I always thought God was male. If he isn't, why do we have all those male words about God in the Bible? And Jesus, too. You confuse me. Wasn't Jesus a man?

A: You make an excellent point. We cannot, dare not, change the pronouns for God or the names and images God portrays for himself in the Bible. But God's role as Husband,

Groom, and Lover to Israel and the Church are important and revealed images. We will likely do serious damage to our understanding of God's relationship with us if we play with Father and turn it into Father-Mother—not so much because male theologians do battle to protect the male images of God as Father and of Jesus as God's Son, but because there are profound images already of the feminine side. "Mother," in God's revelation, is always more accessible, nearer, and more enveloping than Father. And "mother" is always God at work in the God-Spirit-invested community: Israel and the Church. Jesus is historically conceived and born male, grows to manhood, is tried and executed as a male. But in the supranatural cosmic and theological sense, Jesus is the eternal Groom, the second and final Adam, the husband of his Body, the Bride, the Church. His "sonship" is the essential launching pad for his becoming both Bride and Groom: the last Adam.

Q: All of this sounds a little like you have gone over and joined the feminists. Have you sold out to them?

A: The feminist movement covers a wide spectrum, but much of its emphasis is as sexist as male chauvinism has been. As this book unfolds you will see that we are simply unable to find support in Scripture or in the Creation for any "superiority" model of human relationships. Absolute mutual respect and "co-regency" are what Creation and Jesus' call demand of us. We suspect that the Christian church, if it had been faithful to its treasured resources, might have averted the ages-old exploitation of women by men. The so-called "feminist movement" would have been unnecessary, if we had told the truth about Creation and about redemption and had lived out the vision Jesus gave us.

Q: I have heard of an "androgenous Adam." Have I also heard someone talking about Jesus being "androgenous"? Is that what you are teaching?

A: We have no interest in such a term. Some people speak of Adam's being "hermaphroditic," using a word which reflects the combination of Hermes and Aphrodite, a male and a female in the Greek panoply of gods. Today, we all know, a hermaphrodite is a tragic deformity with ambiguous sexual organs. If, indeed, as Genesis two suggests, the complete Adam pre-existed Ish and Ishshah, the man and the woman, we would speculate that Adam was asexual. Indeed, this gives a touch of elegance to the idea that the "image of God" was in that Adam, since none of us is eager to assign reproductive sexuality to God. Asexual reproduction is nonmagnetic, independent of feelings of attraction or attachment based on sexual motivation. And in the several thousand of species God created which are asexual, there is no hint of monstrosity associated with "hermaphrodite" and "androgeny." To suggest that either the first or the last Adam was hermaphroditic or androgenous likely misses the power of the mystery of Genesis two on the one hand and of the Virgin Birth of the Son of God on the other.[23]

Q: If the original Adam was "humankind" and the male and female were formed from that person described in the early part of Genesis two, what kind of a body would Adam have had?

A: When you open the question of the "original morphology" of the undifferentiated Adam, you ask us to go back into physiology and biology. We are less interested in the morphology of the original, undifferentiated Adam than we are the spiritual and theological significance of males and females being made "of the same bone and flesh," hence capable of "having dominion," and of absolute mutuality. As a matter of fact, we can easily accept the "bachelor Adam" interpretation, in which case the Adam body would have been morphologically and genetically male. But there is no hint that the solitary human was "half there" reproductively.

If Adam was designed as an asexual prototype of the original human species, fully able to fulfill the command to "fill the earth" with progeny, then the way is open for "community" to motivate the differentiation of male from female, as Genesis two suggests. But fetal development and actual adult markings suggest that the original asexual reproducing Adam would have had morphology which was capable of reproduction and of nursing the young. Indeed, all male mammals carry the undeveloped but hormonally responsive breasts which characterize the female of the species. Differentiated sexuality may have been a secondary phase of the Creation for all mammals, but it is recorded only for humans, and we think the theological and relational reflections are more useful and important than any other. Those are the reasons we have opened the Bible to Genesis in this chapter.

3

"He Shall Rule Over Her"

△

Polly escaped to Dallas when Dan's misadventures in keeping a mistress at a second apartment surfaced again. Robbie and I had worked with both Polly and Dan, and their anonymous story is part of two previous "bonding" books.

"I'm flying to Los Angeles to do some concentrated teaching in a doctoral program," I told Polly's mother, whose phone number Polly had left with us. "If Polly can get away, I have a three-hour layover in the Delta wing at Dallas-Fort Worth International Airport." I gave her flight number and time.

When I stepped through the arrival gate, there she stood. We moved to my Los Angeles departure gate and sat right there for my entire layover, but I was not prepared for Polly's current theological question:

"Sometimes I think I was wrong to insist that Dan be faithful exclusively to me. When I read about King David in the Old Testament, 'a man after God's own heart,' I notice that he had several wives, even had children by them. And I think, 'That is what Dan wanted, and I wouldn't let him have it. I forced him to choose between Betty and me.'"

Her question stung like an arrow: "Did I do wrong when I

47

insisted that Dan had to be faithful to me or I would have to leave?"

I opened the briefcase I was carrying and took out a tablet of paper. I drew a three-level diagram which compares and contrasts "Creation," "Fall," and "Redemption."

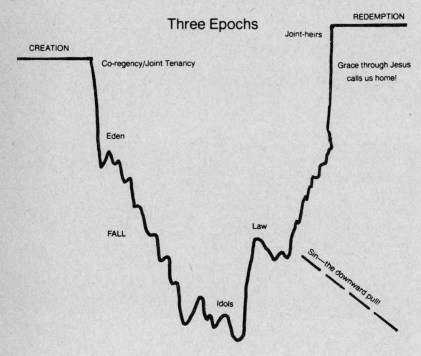

Three Epochs

CREATION

Co-regency/Joint Tenancy

Eden

FALL

Idols

Law

REDEMPTION

Joint-heirs

Grace through Jesus calls us home!

Sin—the downward pull!

"Your dream of marriage is rooted in the Creation. It is standard equipment on all models, both male and female," I told her. Then, pointing to "Redemption," I said, "And Jesus has ushered in a new age in which that Creation dream has been recovered and put within reach again. All sorts of things have been done to eliminate polygamy, murder of unloved spouses, and prostitution to help more and more people claim the dream and have the support of social and political structures for their marriages."

Then, pointing to the chasm denoting the "Fall," I went on: "But King David appeared in history at a time when things were 'in the pits.' God is always able to work through imperfect people. So King David was 'God's man' of the hour for turning the people's hearts back toward faithfulness to their national identity and their earthly mission. But David's life was complicated and his family was devastated by his adultery and by his polygamy. Those tragic features of his fallen culture may never have crossed his mind, since he was trapped in a culture which 'expected' and 'envisioned' the conflicts and pains of polygamy.

"Our problem," I suggested to Polly, "is this. We, too, live in a world that in many ways is still in the grip of the Original Sin. We look around us and see the tragic patterns of sexual behavior and the destruction of families, and it is easy to say, 'So that's normal. I guess my life is not so bad.' And these seductions of our vision can take our eyes off the call to live holy lives in the midst of an unholy world."

I reminded Polly that she was the only one who could say whether her marriage to Dan could survive, that God's vision was for "one flesh, naked and unashamed, for a lifetime." But in no case, I assured her, was she obligated to return "to the pits" of the Old Testament culture which represented the devastating sexual and social consequences of the Fall and to imagine that she would somehow be more Christian to overlook Dan's persistent adulteries.

From Intimacy to Adversaries

From the beautiful images of Creation's marital glue: one flesh, naked, and unashamed, the scene deteriorates to self-indulgent sin. And from the intimacy of the first man and woman "walking with God in the garden in the cool of the day," the relationship with God is fractured by disobedience, rebellion, and their consequences: shame and guilt.

The "Fall" unfolds in this way in the Genesis saga:

1. The Lord God opens the door to creatively manage the whole creation with the exception of "the tree of the knowledge of good and evil [by experience instead of by trust in God's definition],[1] for when you eat of it you will surely die" (2:15).

2. The serpent challenges the man and the woman at the one point of exception: "Did God really say, 'You must not eat from any tree in the garden'?" (3:1).

3. The woman, not Eve but Ishshah, correctly recites the taboo (3:2).

4. The serpent asserts that God has lied: "you will not surely die . . . . For God knows that when you eat of it your eyes will be opened, and you will be like God, knowing good and evil"—by experience instead of by command or intuition (3:4).

5. The woman, softened by the serpent's assertion, observes the visual attractiveness of the fruit of the forbidden tree: It "was good for food and pleasing to the eye, and also desirable for gaining wisdom." She "took some and ate it" (3:6).

6. "She also gave some to her husband, who was with her, and he ate it" (3:6). Contrary to the popular notion that he was somewhere else and didn't know what he was eating once she had removed the fruit from the tree and carried it to him, the text seems clear in saying he was standing right there with her when she took the fruit.

7. "Then the eyes of both of them were opened, and they realized they were naked," (3:7) denotes the awakening of shame, not guilt. Their sudden shock was one of being "exposed," not one of remorse for having violated God's plan for them. Guilt will come generations later. Shame evokes physical, tangible consequences suited for the shallow awareness of the crime; guilt evokes more subjective, inwardly painful consequences, suitable for transforming the guilty sinner into a saint who is in the process of being perfected in righteousness.[2]

8. The shame is intensified as Ish and Ishshah (man and woman) hear "the sound of the Lord God as he was walking in the garden in the cool of the day, and they hid from the Lord God" (3:8).

9. The Lord God calls out, "Adam! Where are you?" (3:9).[3] A loose translation to underscore the solidarity of the original Adam might be to have the Lord God crying out, "Adam! Where are you?" Such a question, in any event, denotes a fracture in the primary relationship with

God. How very different our picture of God would be if he had cried out first, "What is this that you have done?" God's first cry to humans is always one complaining of loss. We were created for intimacy with God. God's search for us is the story of all of human history since the first sin. Any programs of evangelism or outreach which move on any other first principle are not based in the priority of relationships. Those strategies which "use" people, even in the name of the highest religious goals, are deformities of our fallen, violent human nature.

10. In response to God's cry, "Adam! Where are you?" the man answers: "I heard you in the garden, and I was afraid because I was naked, so I hid" (3:10). Here "Adam" is claimed by the man as his exclusive name. The answers are entirely ego-centered and make no effort to explain why the woman may have hidden. Speaking for himself alone, the man names his sin: fear and shame.

11. God offers to convert the shame to truth and thus to free confession of sin: "Who told you that you were naked? Have you eaten from the tree that I commanded you not to eat from?" (3:11). Perhaps all of the history of ego-centered blaming and denial which is universal among our race might have been different if the man could have now told the truth: "Yes. I violated Your command. Was it You who spoke to me from deep inside myself and exposed my failure causing me to see how naked I was?"

12. But the man commits the original act of "blaming," by saying "The woman (Ishshah) You put here with me—she gave me some fruit from the tree, and I ate it" (3:12). The deformed truth comes out: Adam who seems from the text to have watched Ishshah's visual and logical seduction, with no recorded gesture or word of constraint, now attempts to link the "truth" of his sin to her full responsibility. "Blaming" is inevitably an expression of "shame," not of guilt. "Guilt" is preoccupied with telling the truth about the self and assumes that any other person must tell the truth from his or her perspective.

13. The Lord God then turns to Ishshah, the woman: "What is this you have done?" (3:13). Separate opportunities for guilt-based confession and repentance are offered,

but we are not to see maturity here. It is another expression of shame:

14. "The serpent deceived me, and I ate" (3:13). So the moving finger points blame to the serpent whose seductive words awakened the visual curiosity and the chain of disobediences which involved both the woman and the man. The woman's sin was rooted in *deception*. The man's sin, more starkly deliberate it would seem from the text, appears to be willful, sentient, eyes-wide-open *rebellion*.

15. "Eve" is the name the man gives the former "Ishshah," his "bone of my bone, flesh of my flesh" mirror image woman. It is a "functional" name. The naming of Eve is a footnote to the consequences of the Fall, and ushers in the bleak period of human experience in which women were to be regarded as disposable instruments of reproduction and servitude. But more of this later.

Curses and Consequences

What follows, then, in swift succession are three murals depicting both curses and consequences. They apply to the three principals in the crime: the serpent, the woman, and the man. And they appear in the sequence of their active participation in the Original Sin. While the Creation had laid down a solidarity between the man and the woman, and they were jointly charged with tasks of dominion and "filling the earth," their crimes are sufficiently different to require distinct and separate consequences.

The serpent is cursed. Neither the woman nor the man is cursed, only consequences are painted on the walls of their future experience as reminders of their vulnerability to deception and their tendency to rebellion and "willful transgression of the known law of God." The structure and capacity of the serpent is changed, until we likely cannot recognize in any part of the Creation what the serpent may originally have been.[4] It is enough for us to know that an adversary relationship is struck: "I will put enmity between you and the woman, and between your offspring and hers; he will crush your head, and you will strike his heel" (3:15). Check the instinctual response in the back of your

neck and in your pulse rate the next time you overtake a
snake. Our responses to snakes differ dramatically to those
on overtaking virtually any other species. Thus the Genesis
curse on the serpent makes sense to us at an intuitive level
even though the story itself sometimes leaves us baffled,
looking for meaning among the strange images.

The woman is warned. Here there is no curse, only the
cautions that increased pain in the birthing process will
haunt her through time, and that her relationship to her husband will be changed: (1) "Your desire will be for your
husband." But (2) "he will rule over you." At the simplest
possible level, these constraints on the woman may be read as
God's drawing a circle around the possible sexual alliances
she will be able to make. Later both the man and the woman
will be restricted by the anti-adultery law in the Ten Com-
mandments. Unlike the animals which copulate only for reproduction and in many species do so without monogamous
constraint, the humans and especially the woman may have
been tuned for monogamy as a means of protecting them
from the vulnerability of "experimenting" to find "the
knowledge of good and evil." But there is another message
which emerges from the language here. An adversary relationship is struck which is virtually circular: The woman will
be devoted, attached to her man. This will guarantee intimacy of a sort, one consequence of which will be pregnancy.
Indeed, the rhetoric suggests that as the man "rules" her the
woman will be resistant and adversarial. Childbirth will be
so painful as to constitute a true "adversary," filled with
enormous risk, pain, and "the valley of the shadow of death."
But most baffling of all, in all of this attachment, childbearing, and faithfulness, the reward will be an "adversary" husband: "He will rule over you." It is as if God were saying,
"Once you governed the planet as a co-regent at his side.
Now you are going to be reduced to a reacting, adversary
chattel, as he attempts to control everything in sight."

The earth is cursed. At creation, the weight of creative
management of the earth was the conjoint task of the plural
Adam, woman and man together. Now the male grasps that
role as his "reason for being." But the joyous task of transforming the earth and its products into food, structures, and

technology is complicated by the "error factor" of the Fall. Now everything has a central tendency toward chaos instead of toward order. This central tendency appears to spring out of the second curse: "Cursed is the ground because of you— you Adam man" (3:17).

The man is frustrated. Everything is coming up thorns and frustration. Murphy's law is the universal norm: "If anything can go wrong, it will." But all of this teases the male to work harder, to short circuit the Fall, to air-condition his factories and his machines as if to prove that he can roll back the consequences of his sin. But quite inadvertently he has come to regard himself as a mere bundle of brain and brawn. In this reduction in sense of self, he becomes a workaholic, often addicted to debilitating sedatives, drugs, and opiates which numb him through his daily toil and boredom. He forgets that he has emotions and that he was created for intimate relationships. Since he uses himself as if he were a mere "machine," he tends to regard other people reductionistically—also as mere objects to be used, cared for if they have instrumental value to himself, or to be discarded if they only add to his frustration. Everything and everybody is weighed, measured, and evaluated in terms of "their usefulness to me."

The woman is re-named. Ish the male now regards Ishshah, the intimate mirror of Ish, as everything else in his world. She has been reduced to "chattel," not even "real property." She is seen in purely instrumental, self-satisfying terms. Like a machine, or a domesticated animal, she becomes "his property." She is useful, but that usefulness is not described in relationship terms. She is "Eve: the one who makes babies." And here is introduced the tragic beginning of a long history of the reductionistic "instrumentalizing of women." They are chattel, the property of men, and they are disposable: replaceable, if they no longer please their owners.

You Can Have a Marriage Where Everybody Loses!

There is a sense in which virtually every marriage goes through the "idyllic first stage" of mutuality, co-regency, and joint tenancy. But most marriages enter also the "adversarial second stage," of blaming and pushing for one's rights at the expense of the other. And many marriages reach a "final ruptured stage" of abuse, exploitation, and abandonment.

With such a pervasive pattern in romance, the young often wag their heads at their parents and other adults wondering where the mystery of young love has gone. More often, they imagine that the perfect love they are feeling as it awakens must never have been felt by their elders at all. "Poor parents," is the frequent wail of innocence.

And at the cultural level, "living-togethers" sometimes justify their nonmarital living arrangements by defending: "We respect each other too much to embark on an adversarial relationship. Most of our friends showed more appreciation and respect for each other before they were married. We don't want our relationship to deteriorate to that." And when they paint that sort of idyllic scenario most of us feel like we just lost a round of "We gotcha!" What are they seeing in our marriages that evokes so many young lovers to hesitate instead of going all the way to the altar before going all the way to bed?

So let us admit that the "adversary marriage" comes at a very high price. Here is a partial look at the "cost sheet."

1. Power corrupts, and absolute power corrupts absolutely. It may be the husband who becomes domineering and coercive, regarding his wife as "slave" and sex object. But it may also be the wife who resorts to harassment, adding frustration to his world, in order to "use" him as a trophy, a free ticket, or an endless supplier of goods. In any such case the marriage has gone on the rocks with the exploitive use of power. It makes little difference whether the power is musculature, psychological manipulation, or harassment of any sort. We have an adversary model on our hands, and life will drain out of the participants. Their creativity, their long-term goals will all be scaled down to match the dregs of energy which remain to deliver them to their vocational targets.

2. Persons as "property" are imprisoned forever in moral and intellectual infancy. The "kept woman" may be "pro-

tected" by her man, but the fact that she is locked away from the outer world guarantees that she will remain forever a child. Women, taken as a group, suffer a disproportionately high rate of arrested moral and ethical development. The reason, most likely, comes as a direct result of the fact that for the first half of life, many of them have never taken responsibility for their own lives. Many of them have rarely, if ever, made final moral choices, and have not felt the responsibility for handling and interpreting the consequences of tough choices. All of these kinds of responsibilities are essential for advancing through the complex skills essential for higher moral and ethical reasoning.[5]

What I describe here as happening often for women happens also for any social or ethnic group which for any reason is not allowed to take major responsibility for themselves. Children, for example, who are sheltered from decision-making until the age of majority, tend not to be ready to make the kinds of choices which come from "being out of the house." The college freshman year, therefore, is littered with the ruins which follow when adult-aged men and women suddenly have to learn moral responsibility on a grand scale when they never had the "first primer" in taking responsibility for themselves as children. Shared, mutual responsibility becomes critical if the family is to be an environment in which everybody matures and accumulates wisdom.

So the bad news is clear: There is a central tendency in all of us such that our virginal dreams tend to give way to violent adversarial realities. Unless we get a clear perception of the difference between "the way things are" and "the ways things were meant to be," we can be sure that all of us are in for a lot of pain and forfeiture of the best and holiest gifts of life.

In this chapter we have wanted you to weep with us at the enormous losses we all experience, with our First Parents, when we slip into the imitation of the Original Sin. Let us acknowledge that we were made with the vision of Creation in our heads. And let us affirm, too, that Jesus is calling us to recapture that dream through the grace of forgiveness and reconciliation. But let us do the harder thing: Let us now decide to tell the truth in our own marriages, to own full responsibility for our sins against each other, our adversary positioning, and our tendencies to "blame" each other for the failures we hardly have the courage to own as "my fault."

Questions People Ask

Q: For eighteen years, now with several children, I have always known that God loved my husband, and heard him when he prayed. But I have never had any assurance that God cared about me. My husband has made literally all of our decisions, right down to the number of children I would bear. Is it possible that "my desire for my husband" may have set him up to "rule over me" and that is part of the reason that I sometimes don't even feel like a person?

A: You surely may have put your finger on the reason. Self-esteem is not entirely the result of what somebody else does to us, but all of us—men as well as women—suffer from feelings of inadequacy and low self-esteem. Find some trusted person to discuss these issues with, a person who knows you and your family situation. It will be important for your husband's sake as well as yours that you come "on line" with your own direct sense of confirmation and assurance with God.

Q: I am twenty-eight years old and frankly I am a little afraid to date women. It seems there simply aren't any of the old kind left—like my mother, for example. She lives for Daddy and really makes life good for him, and me. I'm still at home. Are you saying in this chapter that there is something wrong with having a woman "take care of you" and devote her whole life to just being your wife?

A: Many women have presented just such a "gift" to their husbands. And there are young unmarried women today, very mature ones, who sense that a vocation of wife and mother is exactly what God has created them for. But a husband and a wife present themselves to each other as gifts. If you are either waiting or actually searching for "such a good functional wife," you are very close to reducing women to "property." And that is a consequence of the Fall and of the curse. But go ahead. Be a man of sanctity and dignity. Look for a good woman who shows also that she is devoted to God and open to relationships based on worth and not on worldly things like looks, money, status, or power.

Q: *There has been a sort of scandal in our city. There was a pastor who led about half of a fine congregation off and started a new independent church. I have noticed that most of the people who went with him are widows, fractured families, and some converted "drug culture" folks. Are some people more vulnerable to "seduction" than others?*

A: We really need research before going further than your kind of speculation. It was significant, however, that when the Jim Jones cyanide suicides occurred in South America there were literally dozens of bodies that were never claimed by family members. Both men and women need significant, safe, substantial relationships in order simply to keep healthy and sane. You can read more about this in the opening chapter of *Bonding: Relationships in the Image of God.* But women, probably because of the effects of the fall, seem more vulnerable than men to "following orders," and are more likely than men to be taken in by an authoritarian figure who "does their thinking for them." But both women and men who come from damaged family systems tend to have problems with authority systems and structures, often craving specific dictated terms. Many of them are very vulnerable to cultic leaders who wish to control people.

4

Intimacy, Trinity, and Family

△

We seem always to be teaching adults and teens about the mystery of human bonding. And when we do a session on "pair bonding," we often talk afterward about wanting to add a thirteenth step: conception-birth of the first child! John was born on December 12, but we never contemplated how meaningful Christmas would be with a new baby in the house. The magic, however, revolved most of all around the sense of completeness that surrounded the house: now we are three! And only last week at Hume Lake with some four hundred people gathered from all over California, one of the couples volunteered the same truth: our marital bond was made indestructible by the birth of our first child. Even couples contemplating divorce seem often to find the baby to be a special kind of "cement" which keeps the marriage together.

Those of us who have grown up around the Christian community have heard the classical analogies about the Trinity. We have had that inexplicable mystery represented to us by the metaphor of water: three forms, ice is solid; water is liquid; steam is vapor, but all three reduce to the same chemical formula. They are "one," but have three forms. There are other metaphors. Then there are triangles and other symbols which evoke mental images of three which, together, form a single entity. Indeed, as we will report here, one classical metaphor of the Trinity is the family.

The Trinity as Community?

A dominant theme which emerges in Creation and remains visible to the final recorded intense prayer of Jesus is one of collegiality, high participation with each other, of intimacy. Indeed, "It is not good that the human should be alone," the divine observation at the creation of the solitary Adam, has the sound of experience ringing through it.

What makes the Father almighty is not some display of archetypal power, but God is almighty because he persistently and passionately is committed to his Creation. He is love and lovingkindness and righteousness; that is the nature of his almightiness. Indeed, in the remarkable exchange between the Lord and Abraham, when Abraham begs for Sodom to be spared, there is ancient text evidence that it was God who "remained standing before Abraham" pleading for the city when Abraham had given up. But our texts seem to have been altered to match our perception that it was God who in a cold and monarchial decree determined to destroy the city.[1]

The glorious power of God the Father, Son, and Holy Spirit does not show itself by seizing power from other competitive forces. Instead, the amazing life-giving power of the Trinity consistently rises out of weakness, not, as Elijah found in the wind, in the earthquake, or in the fire, but in "a gentle whisper."[2] And finally Jesus speaks to us out of the surrender to death itself. And in each case the power expresses itself by collecting communities which appear to be fragile and weak. They are consistently characterized by affection, trust, and order. Thus, the witness of God's power in the world is lived out through those communities, always imperfectly, but nevertheless powerfully.

The great "humiliation of God," namely the downward transformation into the Incarnation of God in human form in Jesus, is taken to its ultimate depths with the death of Jesus. But a further devastation of the divine character is seen when the Spirit of the Father and of the Son carries the redeeming activity of God into the "inbreathing of the Church," the always imperfect image of God which is being called to the likeness of God's character.

We cite these teachings about the Trinity to suggest that community, not power, is the overall image we get of God's activity in the world through Father, Son, and Spirit. But we also point them out to open a window on a central characteristic of God: the complete devotion to relationships without concern for hierarchical structures, roles, or status.

The Trinity as "Family"?

Most of us have a "Westernized" view of God and the Trinity.[3] We see God on the top, Jesus in the middle, and the Holy Spirit dangling below to link us up both to the Son and to the Father. All of this reflects the politics of kings, tenants, and serfs. And our views have been inhaled with the air we breathe in our political environments. Like fish in an environment of water, we rarely contemplate that it might be contaminated—unless, of course, sudden catastrophic circumstances might fling us out of our secure perspective.

It is astonishing that our hierarchical language about God does not come to us out of Scripture, but out of Greek philosophy. Greek "idealistic" philosophy gave us the language of omnipotence, omniscience, and omnipresence to describe the transcendental world of mind and spirit which they held to be superior to our own lesser world of "matter." As Christianity was moving through the early centuries, Christian teachers noted certain affirmations about God's knowledge and dipped into the Greek vocabulary for "omniscience." Then the other "attributes" of God were quickly borrowed from Plato's idealistic philosophy. The roots of all of this verticalizing of the Trinity can be found as early as the second century. Christian thinkers were trying to communicate with the Greco-Roman culture. But from the fourth century on, Plato's concepts were borrowed and filled with Christian content. Much later, as the Middle Ages ended, Aristotle's logical system was integrated into Christian theology, and the shift from biblical categories to a Greco-Roman imperial and philosophical model was fixed.

But contemplate the biblical accounts: God, Jesus, and the Holy Spirit are represented in Scripture as "coming near" to us and as living, themselves, in "community." Both the early (pre-Roman based) church and the continuing "Eastern" church have a global and community view of the Trinity, not a monarchial one. And imagine this! Their favorite metaphor to describe the Trinity tends to be the family: Father, Mother, Child! This, you can see, would give us an inescapable image of "community." What the "family model" for the Trinity will do for us is to give us the message that "to be created in the image of God" is to be placed "in community." It would suggest that any person in isolation may not be "in the image of God." You can see how such a view would rebuke the "privatism" which has given us an all time high in numbers of young adults who are unwilling to enter into marriage, choosing the privatism of the secular "fast lane" social life in preference to commitment, community, and responsibility.

Thus, the "image of God" emerges when Adam is split, and there is no mention of "image of God" except in the context of "male and female." Gregory of Nazianzus declared that Adam, Eve, and Seth are an earthly image of the Trinity.[4] Teachings about the Holy Spirit are highly analogical to the "child" role in the family. The Spirit is the extension of the Father as well as the extension of the Son, for example in Jesus' teachings in John 14–16.

Rome: A Vertical Trinity?

It is easy to see that Western ideas about an imperial Pope modeled on Caesar and a required celibate male clergy both fly in the face of a balanced view of the Trinity as a mystery best understood by relationships in Father-Mother-Child experiences in the family. Ironically both the papacy and the celibate priesthood—which disrupt the Creation model of the family—are labeled with community and family titles: Pope is literally "Papa, Daddy," and the celibate priest is consistently "Father." But the papal pageantry, costuming, and traditional role is that of Caesar—the imperial ruler of a world empire.

And lest independent superchurch adherents among us, or charismatic or traditional Protestants, take too much pleasure in painting the Pope in imperial colors, take a close look at the behavior of your leaders. Dictatorships, let us admit, may be seen in individual locations. Many congregations need not travel to Rome; they may kiss the imperial ring every Sunday. One superchurch pastor answered us when we inquired during a tour of his facility who made up the finance committee:

"You are looking at it!"

Whatever problems you may see in looking at the family as a metaphor of Trinity, and shocking as it is to those of us who have always conceptualized the Trinity in a vertical hierarchy with imperial overtones attributed to the Sovereign One, you must agree that our experience of God and the record of the acts of God in all Persons in Scripture are illuminated by the family image. Many of the power struggles in churches, the splitting of whole denominations, and the general adversary positioning of one group against another "in the name of God" might be greatly modified if we conceptualized the Trinity in community terms instead of imperial ones.

We are always captive to our God images and "act out" our perceptions of God in our moments of highest motivation. Even the relationship between the sexes might be altered toward mutuality if we saw the collected family at the breakfast table as a reminder of the collegiality of God. And the exploitive, imperial sexual adventures of males using females might open the door to a holy kind of intimacy, should we see the intimate community of lovers as God's witness to us of the nature of the Trinity.

"I in Them, as You Are in Me!"

The moving prayer of Jesus recorded for us in John 17 evokes intimate images of the Trinity and calls the church and the family to the unity that comes only in community. For nearly twenty years we have been teaching, using what we have called, "the prayer prayed for you" and emphasizing two things that leaped out of the text:

(1) The prayer for unity assumes the Holy Spirit is present in the community of believers, hence the Trinitarian description which names Father and Son infers Holy Spirit, but names us!

(2) The Trinity thus formulated is one of collegiality and intimacy, and positions the Spirit-charged believers in the role of "Child" related to "Father" and "Mother." The Son, Jesus Christ, is, after all, present and active in the world today as "Body" in the female, feminine form, and we have no hesitation whatever in referring to that representation of Jesus as "she" and "her," even singing about "The Church's one foundation is Jesus Christ *her* Lord."

Look at Jesus' twice repeated cry for "unity," "making them one" petitions in John 17:20–23:

> My prayer is not for them alone. I pray also for those who will believe in me through their message, that all of them may be one, Father, just as you are in me and I am in you. May they also be in us so that the world may believe that you have sent me. I have given them the glory that you gave me, that they may be one as we are one: I in them and you in me. May they be brought to complete unity to let the world know that you sent me and have loved them even as you have loved me.

Now, try to "image" that unity. The Father-Son unity consists of:

Jesus in the Father and the Father in Jesus.

Believers are to have the same reciprocal, mutual, intimate existence:

Believer "a" in believers "x-y-z" and vice versa!

But the imagery moves on to Trinity:

Believers in Jesus and Father, Jesus in all, Father in Jesus.

Remember that the intensive teaching on the Holy Spirit as the inhabiter of human agents is unfolded in previous chapters: John 14, 15, and 16. Now in chapter 17 there is only this climactic implicit teaching which locates the Holy Spirit in the uniting and unified believers who are caught up into intimate fellowship with Jesus and the Father.

In this chapter we have wanted you to look at God's "second curriculum," the Trinity, and to see that the family,

God's "first curriculum for this planet," may also provide us with direct experiences and images to help us understand God. But we have also looked at the possibility that our images of the Trinity may have been deformed by the political environment of Christianity. And to the extent that we have "imperialized" the Trinity, we may also have fed into the hands of the Fall with its curse and consequences. We may have "imperialized" the family as well. If we have, we have done so at the high cost of abandoning intimacy, mutuality, and the high participation of community not only in our families, but likely in our communities of faith as well.

QUESTIONS PEOPLE ASK

Q: Are some denominations or clusters of churches more open to this intimate view of the Trinity and the family than others are? I am so excited about following you through Scripture, but I just know your ideas would be explosive in my church!

A: You may be right. But there is a deep intuitive yearning for truth which tends to cut through any theological system, so if the simplicity of the argument about an "intimate God" and a "Trinity in community" ring true to your experience of God and your reading of Scripture, don't be afraid to own it with the possible consequences.

There may be some theological systems which are more open than others to a theology of intimacy. If so, they could be identified by whether they tended to embrace a "wholistic" theology or simply a "cerebral" doctrinal system. The wholistic churches are those which attend profoundly to the total human being: body, mind, and spirit. The "cerebral" cluster of churches and movements tend to be almost exclusively preoccupied with "words, doctrines, and verbal confessions." The wholistic group is committed to wholeness, holiness of both thought and life, while the cerebral cluster tend to regard the body as evil, without the possibility for holiness in this life, and to center on "orthodoxy" of belief, of doctrinal formulations, and of creedal statements. You will find the wholistic side of the Christian groups interested in evangelism and in hospitals, in biblical authority and in social intervention, and in transformation of culture as well as in eternal life. The more cerebral movement tends to stress verbal assent to doctrines but to be less attentive to holiness of habit and life, to draw the boundaries for "fellowship" based on confessional statements rather than on common experience of Jesus in converted lifestyle, and to require conformity in statements about inspiration of Scripture and of Christ's second coming as a test of admission into the community.

You can see that the "cerebral churches" will not be much interested in the nearness of God or of the model of community and intimacy we have explored here. So look around and see whether you can locate a community which behaves like a community and which embraces the whole of God's call to obedience and to an intimate walk with one another in fulfilling Jesus' call to discipleship in this present life.

5

"Head of the House": God's Order for Families?

△

We were living in Arlington, Texas, in the "Robin Street Parsonage" of a great church there. We had taken official leaves, Don a sabbatical to write, and Robbie a working leave from the elementary schools of Jessamine County. We traded off a Tuesday night intergenerational "family life" series in exchange for the housing, and we pursued our sabbatical projects every morning. The quiet environment gave just the right setting for the birth of the original draft which later became *Bonding: Relationships in the Image of God*.

Three men approached me one Tuesday night after the session to ask whether I would enjoy going with them to a popular men's Bible study at Lovers' Lane United Methodist Church in nearby Dallas—a regular, weekly men's Bible study. Of course I would. So they explained the ground rules. I could go as a guest, but could not participate in the first hour of Bible study unless I had completed my worksheets on the passage for the session. Then, of course, I could be present for the "lecture" by a lay authority trained in California by the founder herself. Finally, I would probably be allowed to pick up the Bible study notes written by the founder. These would be distributed at the door as we left.

All went well. We were looking at the Book of Esther, and the text has intrigued me for many years, though I had never tried parsing it "inductively" as we were trying to do then: seeing it as if we had never seen it or had known its times and traditions before. Then the bright, young Exxon executive mounted the "epistle lectern" in the gracious divided chancel and began to unpack his interpretation of the Book of Esther. It was a fresh and uncritical lecture, I thought. Suddenly, with what might have been a note of slight apology, he struck the "lost chord."

"It is a little embarrassing to note the context," he pivoted in for the blow that would sound the chord itself, "but we have here in chapter two 'God's order for families.'"

And he read it:

> "If it please your majesty, let a royal decree go out from you and let it be inscribed in the laws of the Persians and Medes, never to be revoked, that Vashti shall not again appear before King Ahasuerus; and . . . when this royal edict is heard through the length and breadth of the kingdom, all women will give honor to their husbands, high and low alike." . . . Letters were sent to all the royal provinces, to every province in its own script and to every people in their own language, in order that each man might be master in his own house, and control all his own womenfolk.
>
> Esther 1:19–22 NEB

How It Looks at Home: Don's Story

Chivalry feels good. When I can remember to do it, I like myself better for remembering to treat Robbie like "my little lady," or as "the wife." I like being responsible for her safety, walking on the outside where the howling winds of traffic and any flying debris will strike me first. All of that feels right and I stand tall.

The division of labor feels right too—normal, the way it is supposed to be. My mother always made my bed and gathered my clothes that needed to be laundered. She had my meals ready on schedule. And I rejoiced that such a clean distinction was in place in the universe. Robbie seemed to like doing most of those same things, and I did my part.

My part was to look after everything "external" to the daily household operation. I kept the car clean and lubricated and repaired. I was eager for Robbie to learn to drive and to be licensed—and relieved that my thirteen-year-old sister could teach her there on the farm. But I never expected that she would look after any maintenance of the automobile.

I also expected to be fully responsible for supporting the new marriage and household, earning the income, banking the money, paying the bills, and feeling fully responsible for keeping the supply ahead of the demand. I was built for that kind of responsibility, and it stretched me from being a boy into becoming a man in every sense of the word.

Taking Control of My Woman

Given this enormous "external responsibility" for two people, instead of just myself, I did not hesitate to make decisions for both of us in that outer world. Almost before we were married I agreed to stop off after a week of honeymoon with Robbie to handle all of the music for a three-county summer evangelistic crusade in western Kansas. "And would Robbie be able to play the piano for the event?"

"Of course," I replied, and announced the commitment to her in the next love letter, perhaps six months before the marriage. And she complied. This was, of course, the way I sensed instinctually that things should operate. I knew her. I knew myself. And the external world was my sphere of responsibility.

"Head of the Family"

When the boys were born, four years apart, I initiated the timing of their births. Since I was carrying the checkbook, watching the income, and watching the calendar of our lives, it was clear that the clues from this external world domain would dictate the best time for starting and expanding the family.

Once arrived, it was Robbie, of course, who would look after them, be their primary and largely exclusive care giver. Robbie took a temporary retirement from teaching third grade and did not return to teaching until well after the second son was born. I was glad to be their father, but the care involving feeding, laundry, and bedtime routine were almost exclusively in her corner. The night tending also was her domain—this inner world, caring for the nest, was hers.

I read the headship passages and was warmed. They nourished me by telling me to "love my wife as Christ loved the church," and I resonated with all of that. I found myself formed as a male and all of my militaristic and muscular feelings twitched at the thought of how I myself would lay down my life to protect Robbie and the babies.

I read too of women keeping silent in the church, and that they should never be permitted to teach men. All of this squared with most of what I observed and gradually shaped me theologically into supporting women in the nurturing, child care, and teaching roles in the church. I was then a pastor as well as a public school teacher, and I observed the uncanny way that the women in the elementary school faculty seemed instinctively to know what children needed. It was "mothering" extended to the larger family. But it was men who could handle discipline objectively, act as referees, principals, and coaches. They were dealing with that "external world" and doing it better.

Suddenly, I was given regional, then national attention on subjects relating to family life and Christian education. As early as 1957, I was being flown to regional conferences in my denomination to do teaching. And I was glad to extend the influence of what was working so well in my family and in my church. Then, as an executive in my denomination's educational offices, I could shape the study and conceptual life of a still larger circle. It was then that I completed the work for the Ph.D. at Indiana University. My research project centered on a home and church curriculum experiment.[1] I was not surprised to find that home instruction was as effective as church instruction and when combined they were the most effective of all options. But when I divided the data by sex—after randomizing the sample to eliminate any sex bias—I discovered that boys learned best at home and almost not at all at church, and that girls learned very well at church—almost as well as the boys responded to parental instruction at home. But the girls performed worse with home instruction than either group did at church. That was 1969.

So for nearly ten years I moved ahead on the assumption that the sex difference was indeed a reality. I believed it indicated that the boys needed to learn how to do family headship tasks at home with their fathers, while girls were able to learn their maternal tasks everywhere, especially since virtually all of their church teachers were also women. Incidentally, boys in my sample had almost no contact with male teachers until after sixth grade.

My personal experience was now a professional platform, reinforced by empirical evidence and data. The theory of male headship was nicely formed and readily articulated. I was wrapped in the gentlest of concerns for the protection of women, for the support and cushioning of women from major external responsibility so that their gracious gifts of care-giving, mothering, and loving might enhance the life of both the home and the congregation.

"Control all the womenfolk" in the Book of Esther seemed a bit harsh, I thought, but being head of the home and head of the educational work of the church seemed right. It was so right, in fact, that I seldom thought of articulating it. I found it easy to live it out, to make the decisions I felt were best for the whole family. I surprised them with decisions that involved buying new cars, making travel reservations for vacations which were never dreamed of, even making vocational decisions which uprooted us all. It was tough work, and I found myself needing to bring them around by my logic after the fact of the decision now and then. But they gave me the ultimate affirmation to let me know that this, indeed, was the way it was supposed to be.

I doubt I could have loved Robbie and the boys more than I did in those days before 1971. And our family life seemed effective, even efficient. I did battle "abroad," and Robbie handled the household management. Even when I brought home guests unannounced, she remained well in control. They were strangers brought in from my domain. And my professional obligations sometimes put a claim on hers. We were gracious to each other, obviously lovers in every sense. We reared our family on the second pew front and left, partly because I often had platform responsibility with music in worship, but mostly, I suspect, because that is where Grandpa Joy had sat back in the country church. When we refinished the floor in that rural church there was one visible hole in the paint—the spot where Grandpa Joy sat and patted his foot as he was captivated by the spirit of the music he enjoyed so much.

I was made for this. I was the head of my house. We have never talked about it much, but I'm asking Robbie to tell what it actually felt like to live in this "pater-family," this father-controlled household.

How It Felt at Home: Robbie's Story

In our family with its two daughters it was easy to see Dad as "lord and king." He never demanded special treatment, but he was so different from us three women that his six-foot-two hulk appearing in midafternoon was enough to send us into orbit. He was the "savior of the home" in a literal as well as an ideal sense. He managed to stay up with us till bedtime, read stories to us, even though he was up at 3:30 A.M. and off to deliver Dallas post office mail every weekday. He even permitted us to have a "family bedroom" into our teen years.

My mother has never drawn a paycheck for employment to this day. She ruled the house in some benevolent way, but it was Daddy who was sent by Mother to engage the world, the flesh, and the devil of the world outside. He went to the grocery store. Unwilling to drive a car, evidently because of a frightening early experience, perhaps in Europe in World War I, Daddy offered to buy a car if 'Ree would learn to drive it. So she did. He always took responsibility for its maintenance, but she had to drive it to the station or the garage.

"My Lord, Don"

I could not have been more pleased at moving from the care of Daddy into the total care of my husband. I was glad that he was preprogrammed to paying the bills, and worrying about where the income would come from—or whether we could meet payments should we buy something on time.

What a relief it was to be free to do what I loved to do: to keep house, think about interior decorating, nice touches around the house, and keeping the laundry freshly returned to proper drawers. I didn't need to worry, hardly even to think. It never occurred to me to "decide" about whether I would go to church, to a convention Don was going to attend, to help his parents with harvest time farming. It was enough that Don had considered all of the issues of time, priority, and other moral issues. If he said it, I did it without so much as even a thought of questioning his judgment or the larger issues of whether, like the Creation, the choice was "good."

In the early years when the boys were small, I could count on it that when Don came home from work he would take over. He could make my day simply by walking through the door. I could tell him how exasperated I was and he would walk right into the situation and peace would reign. He could be firm, direct, and the boys would really respond to him. It was like magic. Only rarely was I sorry to have waited for him to solve the domestic crisis, but occasionally he gathered his own data and came out with a different judgment than I had made. In those instances I sometimes felt betrayed, felt he had sided with one of the boys instead of with me. But then omniscience was his gift, not mine, so eventually I would blame myself and we would go on, quite content with our roles.

Deliverance and Protection

My husband was my defender and protector. If, during the parsonage years, I caught some fleck of verbal abuse related to our ministry, he would both soothe me and slay the dragon. And in the early years when the same telephone that came to the parsonage went to the church office, I picked up some calls when he was out. I was proud of him when he informed the secretary of the official board that she was never again to take her anger out on "my wife." And she didn't.

When the decision came to leave public school teaching and to return to school—to theological seminary—I was ready. Don was called to ministry, of course we must go. As the total protector, I recall that he went through all of the channels by which we would be appointed as pastors of the Lexington Free Methodist Church. There were serious "faith leaps" for us, given the lack of parsonage and the minimal income that was likely. When Don announced that the normal three-year program would probably turn out to be five years, and that our income would be so slim we probably could not visit our homes in Kansas or Texas during that time, I felt my first chunk of mild terror. My powerful knight in shining armor was making a decision he had to make—and his options had been reduced to a very small and risky corner. But with a nine-month-old son, Don had determined that I would not work outside the home. So when that immovable object came into conflict with the irresistible force of God's call on Don's life to prepare for ministry, there seemed to be "no other way."

My Liberator

I had to drop out of college after my sophomore year to earn enough money to float our wedding. That was the girl's responsibility, and it never occurred to me to challenge the popular cultural idea of a grand wedding with the cost being borne almost entirely by the bride or her parents. I was seventeen. Don was unable to understand why it would take me out of school, but he knew that my tuition would be his responsibility when we were married a year later. It never occurred to him or to me to discuss my parents' continued support of my education. Don was my provider. His parents could back him and us, if there were any emergency, but I was emancipated entirely from my father's support and care.

And it was Don who kept my dream of being an elementary school teacher alive. He often spoke of my college degree as "our insurance policy on me"—that is, on Don. If he should die, I would not be left without a means of earning a living. His utilitarian reasoning and my vocational dream matched, and I graduated in 1952, only three years after I should have finished with him. And across the years, he continued to urge me on. In Texas, as I was going berserk from cabin fever in a parsonage with one young son and another on the way, he urged me to begin a master's degree program at East Texas State University. My degrees leapfrogged his, and each time, he was urging me on. So when Don began his doctoral study at Indiana University, it was Don's idea that I put my energy where my occasional dream was and complete a "reading specialist certificate." That rigorous program was another thirty hours beyond the master's degree, and we even had a couple of classes together.

Even there, he was my support and my strength. He came to our campus apartment one summer day to find me almost wild as I tried in vain to type a paper for a course in personality theories. Even though he was buried in papers and reading, he transformed my rough notes into a paper so good that the professor asked for a copy to put on the library reserve as a model for future classes. All of that was ironic. And I was deeply embarrassed because Don had written a paper for the same class. It just wasn't right that I should outperform my husband, in his own field, and with the help of his editorial eye and typing.

The Best of All Possible Worlds?

When the man protects the castle and its weak and helpless women and children, how could anything be better or safer in all the world? Everywhere the logic is reinforced. The strong must protect the weak. Women are relatively weaker than men and therefore must be prevented even from trying to protect themselves. Men are larger and heavier and therefore must use their size and strength to shield, to cover, and to care for the smaller and lighter female and her offspring.

A benevolent monarchy is everywhere the most efficient and generous arrangement: the recipients have little responsibility but large reward, depending on the fortunes of the king and on his omniscience in judgments affecting their wealth and comfort. So also the vertical household provides maximum benefits with minimum responsibilities for everybody except good old Dad who brings home not only the bacon, but also the goods and money which are essential to live lives of extravagant consumption and pleasure.

Besides, "good old Dad" loves the role of omnipotent, omniscient breadwinner and pleasure-giver. He feels ten feet tall if he can surprise the family with some good and generous gift, especially if it signals a new level of accomplishment and of success status for the entire family. His annual bonus can buy an extravagant round of Christmas gifts or a special ski holiday for the family. And his "devotion to the cause" of managing the external affairs for the family also justifies his being gone days and nights, most evenings and weekends— he is doing his duty by his family. He takes a second job, or starts up an entrepreneurial sideline, burns midnight oil to get it going, all justified easily because he is improving the quality of life for the woman and children he loves.

Good old Mom tends the home fires, earns her favors by the sweat of her brow as she manages children, runs the car pool, does the laundry, redecorates the house, negotiates with the garbage collection crew over problems in service, collects the bills for Dad to pay, buys the groceries, makes beds, keeps the house immaculate, gets the children's school, meal, and transportation schedules worked out and executes them. She keeps the community safe for children and for herself, helps sell Girl Scout cookies, goes door to door on the drive to build an extension on the public library, attends PTA, sees that the children are in Sunday school or catechism classes, and that the whole family turns up, immaculate, in the Sunday morning pew. And what is most wonderful of all, she does all of this for her husband. It is her gift to him. She adores him, justifies his frequent trips away and out of town, defends him, and considers herself lucky to have his affection, his attention, and his generous backing and financial support.

Dad is unaware of any other possible world of marriage and family, and Mom is oblivious too. It is the apparent eternal pattern from Adam and Eve to Old Testament heroes and modern teachers on family structure in the church. Paul speaks of "headship," so must understand all of this and reaffirm it. And the pattern is everywhere in nature: the animals, the birds, and the bees. And in every primitive society the pattern seems to reappear: men are the gatherers while women bear children and tend the fires at the home base. Of course polygamy keeps popping up in ancient and modern times, but that is not necessarily a sign of any flaw in "God's order for families." Or is it?

Why Does the Vertical Marriage Work So Well?

A sensitive, vertical couple forms an almost indestructible unit. Their expectations of each other match. Conflict is at a minimum. And they can play their roles without asking deep and profound questions about the value of persons, the dignity of personhood, and about the losses they are sustaining by their verticalizing of the marital unit.

But the vertical marriage works well primarily because it matches the fallen configuration of both man's and the woman's personality structure and instinctual aspirations.

Woman: Her "desire" shall be to her husband.

Man: And he shall rule over her.

Work: The male will tend to become a workaholic.

The woman's desire tends to be not only "people oriented" instead of performance, work, or production oriented.[2] Women, taken as a group, tend to have a stronger attachment and dependency relationship to their chosen men. The gift of "subjective attachment" equips her not only to be a mother, but an encompassing source of comfort on a very wide scale. Women tend to be both good listeners and good tellers. They can listen without advising as men are hardly able to do at all. And they have such a high sense of fidelity to friendships that they can be immobilized if they feel they are suddenly placed in a "spot" between two important friends. So the Creation gift of attachment seems to be deformed by the Fall and often turns out to be a fierce and blind magnet which keeps them attached even when they are abused, battered, and destroyed by the relationship.

The man's tendency to rule over her is as instinctual in fallen humanity as her tendency to blind attachment. It is almost as if "he cannot not dominate and control." While women are more subjective and personal in their attachments than are men, men taken as a group tend to hold people, ideas, and issues more at arms length while they deal with them. This "objectivity" is in direct contrast with the woman's gift of subjectivity. But this gift of objectivity—the same gift which describes God as "guiding us with his eye"—tends to turn men into mere machines of observation, analysis, and retooling. Males, compared to females, are preoccupied with "fixing" things. They tend not to be able to listen to people just for the sake of supporting the speaker. Men want to give advice—to treat everything as a problem that needs their objective solutions. And here is the terrible crux of the tragedy: men tend to forfeit their humanity and to turn into machines who process data, make decisions, and put themselves into impossible stress in order to increase their productivity. Men are vulnerable to burnout and to workaholism because of a corrupted tendency described in the Genesis three account of the Fall, the curse, and the consequences.

So why does the fallen marriage work so well? Because it is the "natural and fallen model." It works especially well when both husband and wife are committed to being holy, to telling the truth, and to working at day-by-day reconciliation. When men are made kind, either by training or by God's grace, and when women are embracing a personal covenant which calls for surrender and submission to anyone in authority, their compliance becomes the gift of surrender in the marriage. The kind, benevolent vertical male who is joined with the compliant and affectionate female has formed a glorious "castle for his home." The wife is the queen, and Christ is Lord. And the husband stands between woman and God as her intercessor and her representation of God's supreme role as Husband, Groom, and Father. How could anything so beautiful and so efficient be flawed?

Yearning for the More Excellent Way

I was guest preacher at First United Methodist Church in downtown Tulsa on Father's Day in 1985. Following the third worship service a lovely middle-aged couple lingered to the end of the greeting line in the narthex. Then, taking me aside for appropriate privacy, they confided:

"We joined this church last year because we had come to the end of the rope at a great Bible church in Tulsa. It was because of their teaching about marriage—you know, the 'male dominant' model.

"Somehow we just knew that the teaching was wrong, but they were teaching it from the Bible. And it was a church that surely seems to honor the Bible. Still we knew it was wrong. Our own marriage told us that it was wrong.

"And when we left the Bible church and joined here we did so with a deep sense of loss. We felt that we had to turn our backs on the Bible. But today you gave the Bible back to us."

They were both full of tears by now, as I was, at the thought that fallen men and fallen women are joined by fallen Bible teachers, preachers, and authors who look through fallen lenses until the Scriptures themselves are deformed to teach a fallen view of marriage and the family. And when they have finished their work, they call it "God's plan for families."

I had preached that morning a sermon on "Creation, Adam, and Woman." It is grounded in my book, *Bonding: Relationships in the Image of God,* and is now circulating in a seminar format in the video series, *Relationships in the Image of God.*[3] I could not have preached the sermon before 1980, so I am ready to line up for my medicine along with those who still affirm the vertical household as instinctual and "natural." But I am now ready to ask whether it is God's original design or God's present intention. And when we can answer those questions we may find that in our family relationships as in every other arena, our obedience to Jesus calls us to repentance, repudiation of old ways, and embracing of new and exciting painful learning.

In this chapter we have wanted to show you how well adapted we were for the traditional vertical marriage. We are very much a product of having been through the entire "pilgrimage of our marriage," and this is an important chapter in it.

QUESTIONS PEOPLE ASK

Q: I find your ideas about "co-regency" and your typing your wife's paper very upsetting. My wife is very satisfied with our relationship and we have been trying our best to implement the "chain of command" model which is taught widely in our circles. My wife does the child care and household work like typing, and I earn the living and pay the bills. Why are you trying to confuse the issue when so many people agree with us?

A: We have not written this book to upset anybody—least of all people who are enjoying their "vertical marriages" as we did for so many years. But we discover that there are a lot of people who are ripening in their marriages and in their Christian perspective, and they have serious questions about the popular teaching you mention. Lay this book aside now if it is not the right time for you and your marriage. Get on with your obedience to Jesus, and if you ever have second thoughts about a "control-submission" marriage, you may want to pick it up again. But you must be sure you are ready to trade in your present marriage for a new one called the "Servant-Submission Model."

6

"Chain of Command": The Naturalistic Fallacy Goes to Church!

△

We have been committed to "family priority" since we first contemplated it—even before we were officially engaged. We have practiced that priority, often imperfectly, for nearly forty years. But it was our research at Indiana University which tossed family issues into my professional lap, and my vocation, since 1969, has been chiefly focused on issues related to the family.[1]

In the late sixties an impressive phenomenon began to sweep the country. It was reported to address major family life issues. So in the early seventies we wrote to a certain young leader inviting him to our campus, but his staff responded that he was unable to accept such invitations. It was in the early eighties before his famous seminar reached Lexington. We missed it the first time around, what with all of the flurry of the deadline around our September registration day, but we alerted one of his advocates among our students to keep us on course for "next year." So we bought the registration and made it to Rupp Arena from the beginning of the week-long series.

We were warmed, sometimes confused by the lines of

reasoning, but nicely edified in general. We discovered when examining the Scripture indexes he furnished in the extensive syllabus that his best sessions were the ones with the fewest Scripture references. That puzzled us briefly; then we realized he was often citing dozens of partial verses when propping up a weak session, while his best teaching sessions were those which would nicely unfold one extended passage in its context.

Then about midway through the series the bomb dropped. On the gigantic screen a diagram appeared. It showed a symbol for God, below that a hammer in "strike" position (man) in contact with a chisel (woman) who had strike contact with a jewel (child) being "shaped." We cringed when the diagram flashed on the screen. The videotaped voice of the leader invoked a humorous disclaimer against a literal interpretation of the diagram. But it was his serious words which plunged us into a grief from which we have not yet fully recovered:

"Do you know why a husband and a wife cannot have equal authority in the home?" He was posing the key question. Then he answered it in the most striking way. "It is because 'no man can serve two masters.'"

We were shocked. The implications were enormous. Marriage and family, then, are inevitably locked in conflict. Husband and wife are "competitive adversary masters." What is more, his first teaching about family life zoomed right past the co-regency and joint tenancy, joint-heir images of Creation and Redemption and crashed nose first into the curse and consequences of Genesis three. "He shall rule over her" was turned from God's report of the greatest tragedy of all time into "God's order for families." We found ourselves wondering whether he had ever read that "two become one flesh," and that the design was not merely conventional or friendly cooperation, but actual "uniting of two into one."

But we took you to Rupp Arena for quite another reason. As we sat there in the sports gallery gazing at the video image of the popular family life speaker, a marital fight broke out just two rows in front of us. We have no idea who the distinguished "yuppies" were—two couples of them. We noticed the man directly in front doing some very "hammer-like" jabbing. He was gigging the rib cage of his wife and pointing with the other hand to the image on the screen, as if to tell her that here was the answer she needed. The woman tried to stand up and to leave the row, but he stood up and blocked her, pushing her back into her seat. It was then that the woman, in an awkward piece of high stepping, lifted herself out over the back of her seat and into the empty row in front of us. She sat down alone, obviously shaken. Her husband then stood and in an angry whisper spoke to the other man in the group: "Give me your keys, I'm going to take her out and put her in the car!"

A Naturalistic Fallacy

Suddenly we saw what the speaker was doing. He was blind to the actual teaching of the doctrine of Creation. Instead, he was trying to "baptize" the Fall and to paint a picture of a family which almost exactly reflected back all pagan cultures' views about the relationships between men and women. It was clear that he was sincere and that he thought he was giving us God's view of the family. We got not the slightest hint to suggest that he was aware that his view about male dominance was shared by virtually every stone age culture in the present world, and that it was in the line of descent from which all of us have come. He was taking a measure on what *is* and was concluding that it *ought to be*. He was naïvely committing the "naturalistic fallacy" without giving it the slightest thought.

Scientists and philosophers long ago became aware that they must not jump from *what is* to conclude that it *ought to be*. They know that when they have measured the chemical content of rain water, for example, it may have been contaminated, so you cannot offer a formula from even a large sample of rain water data and say, "This is the way water is supposed to be." Alfred Kinsey would not have been a good scientist if he had studied human sexual behavior and tabulated all of the millions of pieces of data with the intention of announcing what is "normal." He could report all of the statistics and could announce "averages," but he had to stop short of saying, "This is what human sexual behavior *should be*."

Sociologists take great pains to report human behavior. They also take equally great pains to assure us that they will neither make an effort to alter human behavior or to interpret it as normal or good. The naturalistic fallacy fear is keeping them honest.

Where the Naturalistic Fallacy Came From

Who defined the naturalistic fallacy? Philosophers David Hume, G. E. Moore, and Bertrand Russell, among others, have cautioned against falling into the trap of declaring what "is" is what "ought to be." One of the most famous of all naturalistic fallacies is that asserted by the Marquis de Sade. He is sometimes referred to as "the father of modern pornography," and has left his mark in the English language. The term "sadism," used to describe the violent use of other people, is derived from his name. The fallacy he proclaimed ran like this: *Because the human male is stronger than the human female and because males are thus able to do what they will with females, males* should *use their strength to bring females into compliance in any way they wish. Conversely, since women are weaker than men, they* should *be acquiescent in the face of male demands.* The Marquis de Sade went the next step and declared his observation to be "pure natural determinism." Things *cannot be* any other way, since nature has decreed that men are stronger than women.[2]

It is easy to see how pagans of any sort might fall into the naturalistic fallacy, but it is not easy to follow the kind of reasoning by which religious leaders and otherwise very "devout" people can indulge. A pastor near our community tells his staff on Monday mornings to place the guest registrations from the previous day in "temporary file" if they appear to be from divorced, single parent, or black respondents. He may be following a strategy that will successfully fill his fine church with upwardly mobile white members— sometimes classified as building a "homogeneous" church. That is, he has found out what "works" in a fallen and deformed world which is racist, elitist, and naturalistic. But he may have violated *what ought to be.* "Follow up the other guest registrations," he tells the staff, "but we won't cultivate the temporary file."

It is ironic that "the children of this world [the secular scientists] are wiser in their own generation than the children of light." Who would have thought that anyone who saw the bleeding wound stripe of hierarchical power organization crossing every cultural, institutional line would be able to ignore the doctrine of Creation and the message of Redemption and to announce that this deep flaw in the human race is what *ought to be?* How could anyone who was even remotely familiar with the Bible or with history have missed seeing the vision of mutuality in the Creation and noting, in contrast, the tragedy of conflict and adversary positioning which followed the Fall?

Blow the Whistle on the Naturalistic Fallacy Offenders!

Adversaries, hustlers, and pornographers, to name a few, make it their business to seduce everybody into thinking that "everybody's doing it; therefore it's both cool and 'right'!"

Since about 1970, for example, USA citizens have been told that everybody agrees that a little soft pornography is really quite innocuous, and everybody looks at it. So the piles of explicitly sexual magazines have stood near the cash registers of thousands of stores and shops and we have all been assaulted with the material until it was easy to believe that "because it is everywhere, it is wanted and somehow acceptable and 'right.'" Suddenly it turns out that everybody never did want the stuff. We were being sold an "invented" story by the hucksters who must have wanted our money or our integrity. And it is embarrassing that it took so long for us to find our voices and ask whether, indeed, "everybody's wanting it."

Lying in advertising is a national scandal. It is so comical that almost any real story of the rise of a new product would read like pure fiction. Yet we tend to believe the ads. Lee Iacocca can bring Chrysler back from the verge of bankruptcy simply by making a television commercial and pumping us into his dealerships. Yet Chrysler products are still genetically the same as before. Madison Avenue "fluff" has struck again, and it has created the impression that something was true when business was still as usual. This first cousin of the naturalistic fallacy, I want you to see, is our national pastime. We love to be lied to—to be told how "millions" of people have avoided bad breath or have found new "sex appeal," when as a matter of empirical fact, nothing of the kind has happened. Here the "data" is so often a matter of pure invention that a national agency has to watchdog the advertising world. Instead of reporting "what is," they have a tendency to invent pure mythology and to pass it off as truth.

It is easy to see the "fallacy" of advertising, but most of us are easily seduced by so-called "research findings." We do a bit of research ourselves, and the first rule of any careful researcher is that the findings must be interpreted only as representing the "sample" that was chosen. We have studied a random sample of children of grades four, five, and six, in the Southern Michigan Conference. We have also studied forty-three ministers attending a continuing education seminar. And more recently we have taken sexual experience data on a class of forty-one of our students. Now, we are irresponsible reporters if we violate two rules: #1. Inferences must be from the sample and may not be generalized to wider populations which may have different characteristics. #2. Findings must be regarded as measures of *what is*, and must not be interpreted as any sort of "standard" or justifying yardstick to suggest what *ought to be*.

If we found that ministers are abusive to their wives and children, we could not then infer that all men indulge in this sort of sin. You would not let us get away with a research analysis which suggested that ministers ought to be expected to be abusive since we found a high percent to be handing out abuse. Nor would you want us to announce that "men ought to abuse their wives because a large research group of ministers shows a high percent of abuse in their marital relationships."

Magazine surveys and so-called "scientific reports" are everywhere. We read *Redbook*'s[3] report on 100,000 women, or the famous *Hite Report*[4] on women and men, or Robert Coles' *Sex and the American Teenager*.[5] And we assume that we are, indeed, reading "what is." Far be it from *Redbook* or Shere Hite or Robert Coles to go so far as to say, "Read our reports and 'go and do likewise,' since 51% of our respondents do it." Even when they abstain from the suggestion, it is easy for us to read their reports and make the "ought to do it" leap.

And here is the intrinsic danger in all of our empirical studies and reporting. However honest we may be in limiting our work to "mere reporting of what is measured," many people who hear us or read us are likely to justify their leap into the practice of the measured behavior on the basis that 75 percent of the people Joy reported on "do it."

But the real shocker with *Redbook*, Hite, and Coles, whom we choose arbitrarily, because we read their reports and are thankful that they took the trouble to do research and to report, lies here: The researchers ask important questions of the "samples" available to them. But they do not begin even to measure "what is." They are flawed by the nature of the selection of their samples. *Redbook* and Hite used "volunteers." Coles polled 3,000 homes which were contacted through *Rolling Stone* magazine. This household sample may already have a "bias" on matters of sexual behavior. Coles had to settle for a little more than one-third of the three thousand homes he contacted in the actual research. Yet he reports his findings and has the courage to call the report *Sex and the American Teenager!* The research method has failed to give us a valid "probe" even into the *Rolling Stone* population, not to mention the general population. No other kind of empirical research would take seriously the kind of biased sample these reports present.

And herein lies a serious possibility: We may be given these reports with the authors' and publishers' intent of seducing public morality by suggesting that people who volunteer for sex research are "normative," "average," "typical," in order to erode the fairly healthy public moral sense about sex. Can you speculate why two thirds of Robert Coles' *Rolling Stone* survey sample may have refused to complete the research procedure? What if the missing two-thirds of Robert Coles' *Rolling Stone* survey sample represents the general public better than the 1,000+ who accepted the invitation to be studied? That silent "no" group may, in fact, hold that (a) details of their teenagers' sexual behavior are private, (b) to invade that privacy would be to suggest that they are mere "objects" to be measured, and would likely (c) contribute to the devaluing of their worth as persons, and to (d) trivialize sexuality, with a likely effect that they would feel some obligation to be more sexually active than they may be.

So much of what appears to be good reporting of what is may in fact be flawed. A "hermeneutic of suspicion" needs always to raise the question of whether the research sample or method is seriously flawed. If we are short of more valid research, we may find ourselves wanting to attend to flawed reporting, but feeding in a "correction" when we interpret what we are reading. But in any case, we must always join the scientific community in applying their own rule: beware the naturalistic fallacy.

Checking to Detect the Naturalistic Fallacy

People in the Judeo-Christian traditions should not need to be told that *what is* is very often exactly what *ought not* to be! Let us offer some touchstones and a set of guidelines for checking any piece of evidence that seems compelling.

Let's take Hume, Moore, and Russell seriously. None of us is going to live long enough to get the "big picture" of reality. One has only to read a little history or pay attention to the newspaper to see how complex the human scene is. And when we contemplate the span of centuries, we see how easily we get trapped into "the present moment." "The present culture" is even more sticky quicksand. A proper humility should strike us when we attempt to generalize from any is, declaring it to be a universal ought.

Now, we can look in all of these directions and become paralyzed. The pure "existentialist" tends to be frozen by the idea that no perfect virtue, no absolute value exists, and that every person must be at liberty to go into oblivion in some personally satisfying way.

Elsewhere we have outlined what we call "the three witnesses" whose perspective we need to verify any idea, value, or description of reality.[6] Those witnesses are (1) Creation,

(2) Scripture, and (3) Jesus. When looking for error it is important to look at a fourth, (4) Sin and Fall.

In Chapter 3 we spread the diagram of history across the page to illustrate how Creation, Fall, and Redemption represent three major epochs by which to take a measure on where we are today in our perspective on the family. Using such a "road map" we then can test the *is* and speculate about whether it might be *ought*. Let us reprint the same diagram here so you can locate the "trap" which gets us into the "naturalistic fallacy."

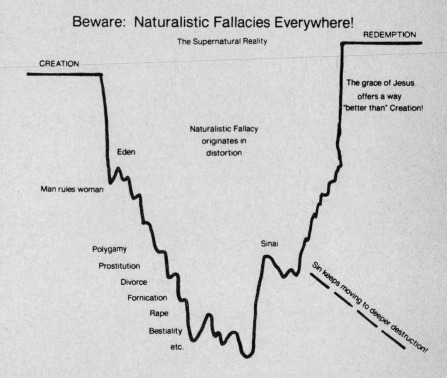

Beware: Naturalistic Fallacies Everywhere!

If we could take a sample of human vision, aspiration, or behavior from the period designated "Creation," we might, indeed, find that it matched "what ought to be." We can read the first two chapters of Genesis, but we even read them with "fallen eyes," so that we read back into Paradise motivations, fears, and biases that are foreign to the circumstances reported. Test points from Creation include these: Is self-interest motivating the behavior? Are the participants indeed innocent? Do the relationships between humans and between humans and the natural environment make for harmony, balance, ecological wholeness? Is there obvious order, design, and balance? Does the "motion" take the entire set of participants toward mutual fulfillment, peace, and higher sensitivity to all that is whole, balanced, and harmonious?

But if we planted our test station in the Chaos which has characterized history since the Fall, we would likely find both human relationships and ecological connections which *are*, but of which it must be declared, they *ought not to be!* Here are some test points: Is "progress" for one person or one group at the "expense" of another? Is behavior motivated by personal profit, gain, or acquisition of power over other people or objects? Does the piece of human motivation or behavior we are looking at lead to mutual wholeness or toward pain, jealousy, arrogance, or destruction? Is there a "price" and "payoff" involved in the transactions? Who is asserting the rights of privileges—those who stand to benefit from the exercise of the rights or those who stand to pay for them?

Now, try planting our experimental station in Redemption. Since Jesus is here and the Second Adam has shown us what life was meant to be, we will expect to find major perspectives which are harmonious with Creation and which are in contradiction with human perspectives in Fall and Chaos, even when enlightened by Law which was a temporary repair getting us back in touch with God's vision for us. But there are problems taking a sample from the Redemption soil, too.

Redemption denotes the section of the diagram where God's character is written in some people and not in others, so all human relationships are carried out in a contaminated environment and between "unequals." And, what is even more tricky, God's redemption is at work in various ways in various people, some responding to more of God's character than others. So, a sample of "humans under reconstruction" is not a safe measure. Some test points, again, might include: Are the relationships mutually enriching and ennobling to everybody involved? Are the implications for all of the environment "constructive" or just not "destructive"? Are there special benefits to any person or group of people at the expense of another person or group? Is there anything intrinsically demeaning in the sample of behavior? Are the participants transparently honest, open, and holy—the moral equivalent of Creation innocence?

In all of this search it is critical that the three legs of the tripod be firmly shaken down to solid footing: What is implied from Creation? What does Redemption say? And when Scripture reports all of these, can we see some revealing light in the tragedy of the Fall or in the face of Jesus? These are very likely to turn our lenses toward the highest reality. And throughout this entire book we are wanting to look at all of the data, examine and weigh the words and the conceptions as we reach out to answer the question, "Whatever happened to Eden?"

So here is our formula: Anchor the tripod of your "scope" on Creation, Scripture, and Jesus. Then look for a "match" between anything you observe today—*what is*—and a corresponding instance from one of the three periods in the time line: Creation, Fall, and Redemption. For any piece of evidence of what "works," take it to (a) Creation, (b) Redemption, and cross reference it against (c) the Fall.

Why the Chain of Command Works

If anyone could make a "chain of command" work, it would be Christians. Likely they have learned it from the Jews who have survived violent repression and efforts of genocide across the centuries. All that is necessary for the chain of command to work is the acquiescence of the people on one end of the polarity. We will not be surprised in any situation, whether it is a political system or a marriage, that the more powerful and affluent end of the spectrum demands unilateral submission, not infrequently using illegitimate means to achieve the desired compliance. Unilateral passivity will guarantee that the chain of command will work in any situation and for any cause.

Curiously, Scripture nowhere requires women to "obey" men, though children are required to "obey parents." The "submission" obligations are everywhere, but they are bilateral, not exclusively required of women. "Submission," as we will see in Chapter 8, "Head and Body: The Complete Adam" is the distinctive grace-based option for all believers.

Unilateral submission and its partner, unilateral use of power, present a quiet tragedy. When passivity and obedience is the pattern it tends to be fed by a "roll over and play dead" attitude. In the early stages, the passive victim often retreats inward with some hostility or pouting. Eventually, as the intellectual energy atrophies from lack of use, a distinct price is paid in moral and mental rigor. People who need not make decisions tend to lose the capacity to do so. Many women have been reduced to a "childhood mentality" by the chain of command. The tables can be turned, of course, and a domineering woman can turn any man into a boy. The point is, the chain of command comes at a very high price. But it "works," if silence is the premium one wants around the house.

In this chapter we have wanted you to ask the question, "Where did we get the 'chain of command' idea for marriage and the family?" We wanted you to consider that it may be a legacy of the Fall and was never intended as God's order for families. We wanted you to play out some implications of believing that we can prove "what ought to be" from looking around to see "what works." If you have done that, then you must be walking with us toward that vision of what God is calling us to come home to by grace. It will take a miracle, of course, if we are to be restored to the image of God, but then that is the gracious offer God holds out to us. First the Original Adam, then the Second Adam, but after Jesus, a whole line of recreated Adams is forming. And we are they: male and female in the image of God. We have been bold to announce the final chapter of this book as "The New Adam: From Image to Likeness."

QUESTIONS PEOPLE ASK

Q: *My pastor taught me the "chain of command" concept and I practiced it the best I knew how with my husband. But it seemed to actually backfire on me, and my husband began to run around on me. Eventually he demanded a divorce, and now I feel really cheated. I think my husband respected me less and less until he just "threw me away." Why would the chain of command backfire?*

A: Nobody can see the heart of another person, so there may have been very complicated and evil reasons why your husband left you. But it is true that passive acceptance of neglect or abuse often has a double effect: #1. The abused or neglected spouse tends to gradually lose respect for the offending spouse, finding a decline in the magnetic attraction toward the negligent or abusive spouse, and to a hardening of affection—the heart. #2. Lowered self-respect in the passive spouse, leading to less attractive behavior and appearance, thus provoking more and more neglect or abuse. We want to look at "submission" and "servanthood" in a later chapter, but they must be carried out with dignity and self-respect or they miss their intended service and become almost suicidally self-destructive.

Yes, we can imagine that the "chain of command" may have destroyed your marriage. We grieve that so-called "conservative," even "evangelical" husbands may also be more prone to abuse than husbands in the general population. Dr. James M. Alsdurf, in a doctoral dissertation entitled *Wife Abuse and Christian Faith: An Assessment of the Church's Response,* published at Fuller Theological Seminary in 1985, offers painful evidence. Not only does abuse occur and seek out justification in Scripture, pastors tend to offer advice which they base in Scripture to justify accepting the abusive structure in the marriage.

We note, too, that some new Christians are so "deformed" by their communities and their own intense preoccupation with being "good parents," that they are prone toward doing violent things to their children in the name of Christian discipline. Our conclusion is that we must read the large message of Christian faith and note that violence in relationships always is rooted in evil, not in God.

7

On Silencing Women in the Church

△

Julia Arnold Shelhamer was a legend in our denomination long before we actually met her. Then she moved from Washington D.C. to "retire" at Winona Lake, Indiana, where we lived and worked. That was the late sixties and she must have been in her eighties.

"How do you like living at Winona Lake?" Dr. J. F. Gregory, another longer-term headquarters personality asked her one day.

"Very well, but I miss the drunks," Julia answered casually. She had moved from Washington D.C. and her street ministry which was widely known and respected. She is credited with operating the first "dial-a-prayer." It consisted of her number in the phone book, with a "live" Julia on the other end of the line, listening, counseling, and praying with the anonymous callers.

Mrs. Shelhamer preceded us in moving from Winona Lake to Wilmore, Kentucky. Her son-in-law, the late Dr. Gilbert James, was our colleague and mentor. He had been a flaming evangelist from our separate childhoods, and was settled here as a sociologist and respected "urban ministries" trainer. We saw her to her 101st year and joined a gathering of celebrants for the final memorial service honoring her going home.

Julia was a world class woman. On her ninety-sixth birthday she spoke in chapel at Oakdale Christian High School in Breathitt County, Kentucky, a favorite school of hers. There the students were overwhelmed with her persistent Christian service. It was in about the same year she preached a ten-day revival in Watts, Los Angeles.

Esther James, her daughter, provides some amazing data on this remarkable woman:

At the age of thirteen Julia was impressed with God's call to Jeremiah in chapter one, and felt that verses 4–9 applied also to her. Since helping to bring people into a right relationship with God was the only important business of life, every available evening was spent attending revivals or assisting in street meetings in Chicago's saloon and red light districts. At seventeen she was asked to speak every Wednesday night to large numbers of derelict men at Olive Branch Mission, and before her marriage at twenty-three she had received calls to assist in revivals in several Illinois churches.

At about eighteen she was prevented from receiving an evangelist's license from a certain official board by a leading board member's loud denunciation of women preachers. Naturally she keenly felt the rejection, even though she had not asked for the license. Her friends then went through other legal channels and secured for her a license from the district quarterly conference. Much later in life, after preaching in nearly every state and on two missionary trips around the world, she was ordained deacon. She says,

"A few times in my life we have met men who openly and strenuously opposed the idea of a woman preaching the Gospel. This once greatly troubled my reticent spirit, but I have learned to go right on as though there were no opposition. Time is too short and God's work too important to stop and parley with opposers. I notice that such men are doing little if anything toward aggressive evangelism. It is not my business to offer an apology to them for the commission given to me by the King."[1]

Another biographer described Julia:

Through the greater part of a century, [she] would give herself without reservation to the physical and spiritual welfare of others—a tiny enthusiastic woman, who twice would encircle the globe with the gospel, raise hundreds of thousands of dollars for the underprivileged, be invited up from her little mission to sit at breakfast with the President of the United States, and whose remarkable ministry among the suffering would be featured in *Time* magazine. And greater than these things, her humility and simple faith in God could not be destroyed.

He described her preaching:

Without yelling she made them hear; without weeping she brought tears to the eyes of wicked, wretched men; without resorting to any of the tricks of the profession she invited sinners to the altar, and they came, weeping, repenting, believing, and were saved.[2]

Although Julia's denomination finally got around to granting full ordination to women, she managed to keep faith with the call of God on her life in spite of the opposition of some people to licensing and ordaining her.

Doesn't Everybody Agree?

There is an amazing thread of Scripture which seems to suggest that the traditional "male control" of leadership is the will of God, even the design of the creation. Look at the excerpts with which we can construct a male-leadership design:

Now I want you to realize that the head of every man is Christ, and the head of the woman is man, and the head of Christ is God.

1 Corinthians 11:3

As in all the congregations of the saints, women should remain silent in the churches. They are not allowed to speak, but must be in submission, as the Law says. If they want to inquire about something, they should ask their own husbands at home; for it is disgraceful for a woman to speak in the church.

1 Corinthians 14:33–35

Wives, submit to your husbands as to the Lord. For the husband is the head of the wife as Christ is the head of the church, his body, of which he is the Savior. Now as the church submits to Christ, so also wives should submit to their husbands in everything.

Ephesians 5:22–24

A woman should learn in quietness and full submission. I do not permit a woman to teach or have authority over a man; she must be silent. For Adam was formed first, then Eve. And Adam was not the one deceived; it was the woman who was deceived and became a sinner. But women will be kept safe [be saved] through childbirth, if they continue in faith, love and holiness with propriety.

1 Timothy 2:11–15

Likewise, teach the older women to be reverent in the way they live, not to be slanderers or addicted to much wine, but to teach what is good. Then they can train the younger women to love their husbands and children, to be self-controlled and pure, to be busy at home, to be kind, and to be subject to their husbands, so that no one will malign the word of God.

Titus 2:3–5

Wives, in the same way be submissive to your husbands so that, if any of them do not believe the word, they may be won over without talk by the behavior of their wives, when they see the purity and reverence of your lives. . . . For this is the way the holy women of the past who put their hope in God used to make themselves beautiful. They were submissive to their own husbands, like Sarah, who obeyed Abraham and called him her master. You are her daughters if you do what is right and do not give way to fear.

1 Peter 3:1–6

To the woman he [the Lord God] said,
  "I will greatly increase your pains in childbearing;
    with pain you will give birth to children.
  Your desire will be for your husband,
    and he will rule over you."

Genesis 3:16

Here we have it, and we have it all—in twenty-two verses. The sum of the clear teachings of these scriptures is this: Women are to regard men as "head," to be submissive to them, to be silent in church—depending on childbirth as their special means of salvation grace and never teaching or having authority over men, to teach younger women, to stay at home, and to obey and be ruled by their men.

Is the "Curse" God's Will for Women?

Here is the most obvious and most tragic flaw in our long-term and energetic efforts to polarize the male and female values, demoting woman to inferior status and privilege. Look at the passages which revolve around possible "inferiority" of women:

> To the woman he [the Lord God] said,
> "I will greatly increase your pains in childbearing;
>   with pain you will give birth to children.
> Your desire will be for your husband,
>   and he will rule over you."
>
> Genesis 3:16

> Likewise, teach the older women to be reverent in the way they live, not to be slanderers or addicted to much wine, but to teach what is good. Then they can train the younger women to love their husbands and children, to be self-controlled and pure, to be busy at home, to be kind, and to be subject to their husbands, so that no one will malign the word of God.
>
> Titus 2:3–5

> Wives, in the same way be submissive to your husbands so that, if any of them do not believe the word, they may be won over without talk by the behavior of their wives, when they see the purity and reverence of your lives. . . . For this is the way the holy women of the past who put their hope in God used to make themselves beautiful. They were submissive to their own husbands, like Sarah, who obeyed Abraham and called him her master. You are her daughters if you do what is right and do not give way to fear.
>
> 1 Peter 3:1–6

The Genesis material is simply a record of the consequences of the original sin. It is not the decree of God or the announcement of God's design. Quite the opposite: the statement is a caution, a warning that women will tend to be blind to the imperfections of their men, to be overly reverential toward them, to adore and worship them to their own detriment and that of the entire human race. Then there is the stinging further caution: men will accommodate your own deformity by "lording it over you."[3]

In the Titus and Peter material above, it will be important to ask whether the advice the authors are giving would apply equally to "older men," and to all men in general who were seeking to live godly lives. The principles are both simple and profound:

(1) Show respect/reverence all around. (2) Teach those younger than you, especially those who are likely to be going over the "same curriculum" as you, those of the same sex and probable vocational destiny. Finally, (3) remember that "servanthood" and submission are always the first Christian response, and that in a conflicted situation, know that nonresistance and graciousness are always the Christian's distinctive trademark.

Peter and Paul: Early Church, New Testament Principles

It would be near-sighted and self-serving to read any of these texts as "assuring males of their right to have submissive, reverence-giving, roll-over-and-play-dead women," or to make those behaviors a test of the women's faithfulness to God. Both Peter and Paul go over the edge to demand of all Christians that they love one another, respect one another, surrender to one another, and forgive one another. These higher priority claims must be applied first and most rigorously. When they are made the target of Christian living, the silly arguments about who has power, authority, or privilege disappear. To the extent that anyone is preoccupied with "proving the superior or inferior status" of men or of women, we may be absolutely sure that they have surrendered the heart of the Christian vision. Because at its heart lie the core teachings. Listen to the apostles:

Peter, on the Day of Pentecost:

> Fellow Jews and all of you who are in Jerusalem, let me explain this to you; listen carefully to what I say. These men

are not drunk, as you suppose. It's only nine in the morning!
No, this is what was spoken by the prophet Joel:

> "In the last days, God says,
> I will pour out my Spirit on all people.
> Your sons and daughters will prophesy,
> your young men will see visions,
> your old men will dream dreams.
> Even on my servants,
> both men and women,
> I will pour out my Spirit in those days,
> and they will prophesy.
> I will show wonders in the heaven above
> and signs on the earth below
> blood and fire and billows of smoke.
> The sun will be turned to darkness
> and the moon to blood
> before the coming of the great and
> glorious day of the Lord.
> And everyone who calls on the name of the Lord
> will be saved."

Acts 2:14–21

Peter, picking up the Creation vision and announcing it as redemption's vision, uses the words of the prophet Joel[4] to announce the "almost, arriving, but not yet dominant" consistent will of God:

1. *All people:* traditional racial distinctions are ended.

2. *Sons and daughters prophesy:* sex distinctions are erased.

3. *Young and old . . . :* age discriminators are abolished.

4. *Men and women,* literally "maid servants" and "men servants": social and gender distinctions are abolished.

Paul, on Christian Initiation:

> You are all children of God through faith in Christ Jesus, for all of you who were baptized into Christ have clothed yourselves with Christ. There is neither Jew nor Greek, slave nor free, male nor female, for you are all one in Christ Jesus. If you belong to Christ, then you are Abraham's seed, and heirs according to the promise.

Galatians 3:26–29

Here, Paul joins Peter in detailing the transformations that are to be expected in the Christian community:

1. *Neither Jew nor Greek:* racial differences are erased.
2. *Neither slave nor free:* social, political, and class differences are abolished.
3. *Neither male nor female:* value based on gender is ended.

With these sweeping "general rules" announced by both Peter and Paul, it will be important to take any single specific statement from any other text and ask how it may be interpreted in the light of the generalizations here.[5] Take a case in point. Look at the passage in 1 Peter again:

> Wives, in the same way be submissive to your husbands so that, if any of them do not believe the word, they may be won over without talk by the behavior of their wives, when they see the purity and reverence of your lives. . . . For this is the way the holy women of the past who put their hope in God used to make themselves beautiful. They were submissive to their own husbands, like Sarah, who obeyed Abraham and called him her master. You are her daughters if you do what is right and do not give way to fear.
>
> 1 Peter 3:1–6

Anyone seeing the language of the opening line would certainly wonder what Peter means by the words, "in the same way . . . ."

"In the same way" refers back to the case of Jesus who suffered for doing good and endured it. "When they hurled their insults at him, he did not retaliate; when he suffered, he made no threats. Instead, he entrusted himself to him who judges justly." And the case of Jesus is to illustrate a principle Peter is teaching about how to relate to the pagans, to "every authority instituted among men: whether to the king, . . . or to governors . . . . For it is God's will that by doing good you should silence the ignorant talk of foolish men. . . . Show proper respect to everyone: Love the brotherhood of believers, fear God, honor the king."

Another case to which "in the same way" may refer is that of slaves. "Slaves, submit yourself to your masters with all respect, not only to those who are good and considerate, but also to those who are harsh . . . ." So Peter is drawing "the worst case," and is then advising women in the Christian community who may be receiving the "worst treatment." In Peter's congregations, as in many of ours, the abused, virtually abandoned women and mothers needed comfort, support, and the special teaching which might help them cope with a spiritually fractured household. The advice to women is almost entirely one of suggesting how, unilaterally, to "make a difference" by practicing the general policy of submission. Try to imagine how a Christian husband might have received the teaching to the woman, had he been seated beside her or reading the letter over her shoulder. It is clear that this is a message addressed to women in the absence of their husbands—the Christian woman's secret strategy offered by counselor, advisor Peter. Yet, today it tends to be males who are obsessed with demanding unilateral submission by women.

Ironically, husbands get the final treatment in the series. Paul in Ephesians moves from "both," to wives, to husbands, to children, to slaves. Here Peter moves from: all submitting to kings, slaves submitting to masters, Jesus submitting to torture, wives submitting to husbands, to husbands elevating their wives: "Husbands, in the same way be considerate as you live with your wives, and treat them with respect as the weaker partner and as joint-heirs with you of the gracious gift of life, so that nothing will hinder your prayers" (1 Peter 3:7).

The husbands have been under joint orders to submit to external authority and to those who abuse when you are acting righteously. Henpecked husbands have already had their strategy of submission outlined in the Jesus model ahead of their single verse. But something new is added, and it is a vision right out of the Creation. There, the man and the woman were co-regents, joint tenants, of the planet. Now, Peter reminds them, they are joint heirs of the gracious gift of God's redeeming new life. All of this is couched in the language of consideration, of absolute respect, of protecting with superior musculature, but of equality of footing in the receiving of God's grace.

Then, a final caution closes the brief advice to husbands:

be careful to do all of this "so that nothing will hinder your prayers." Is this a magic formula for getting your prayers answered? Likely not, but imagine how gentle all of us men would be if we realized that our moral and spiritual character is clearly a fraud if the acid test of "spouse treatment" turns out negative!

Submissive Wives?

Of course; but women are obligated to submit only because all Christians are called to exercise the first option of God's grace. Servanthood and submission are synonyms and thus connect Gospels and Epistles in a conceptual fabric which is often ignored. The grace of servanthood may be a gift of love in good times and a deliberate strategy of constraint in tough circumstances. Should we check the context for Paul's teaching? "Wives, submit to your husbands as to the Lord. For the husband is the head of the wife as Christ is the head of the church, his body, of which he is the Savior. Now as the church submits to Christ, so also wives should submit to their husbands in everything" (Ephesians 5:22–24).

The "submission" discussion has been introduced with a listing of Christian behavioral demands.

> Be imitators of God, therefore . . . and live a life of love, just as Christ loved us and gave himself up for us . . . . Among you there must not be even a hint of sexual immorality . . . . Have nothing to do with the fruitless deeds of darkness, but rather expose them . . . . Be very careful, then, how you live . . . making the most of every opportunity, because the days are evil . . . . Do not get drunk on wine . . . be filled with the Spirit . . . . Speak to one another with psalms, hymns and spiritual songs . . . . Submit to one another out of reverence for Christ.

Then follows "Wives, [submit] to your husbands as to the Lord." Paul is clearly making this the first of a series of "submissions" which will follow.

Husbands have a submission obligation that is unique to them: "love your wives, just as Christ loved the church and gave himself up [died] for her to make her holy, cleansing her by the washing with water through the word, and to present her to himself as a radiant church [wife], without stain or wrinkle or any other blemish, but holy and blameless."

Children submit, too. "Obey your parents in the Lord for this is right."

Fathers submit by not exasperating their children; "instead, bring them up in the training and instruction of the Lord."

Slaves submit. "Obey your earthly masters with respect and fear, and with sincerity of heart, just as you would obey Christ." "Obedience" is called for from slaves and from children, not from wives or husbands to each other.

Masters submit. "Treat your slaves in the same way [as you do your children]. Do not threaten them, since you know that he [God] who is both their Master and yours is in heaven, and there is no favoritism with him."

This is circular submission, a sort of "dance of servanthood" which is played out by equals under the loving eye of the creating God who "loves us all the same." Of course, submission is a Christian pattern, but it knows no special class, sex, or status group on which to focus.

Denied Authority, Saved through Childbirth?

Here is a remarkable package of potential doctrinal teaching. If this were all we had of St. Paul, we would have to redefine the doctrine of original sin as well as our doctrine of salvation by faith alone. After these, we could then move on to generate a doctrine of male-female relationships. It stands in shocking contrast to two clear teachings everywhere else in history and Scripture: (1) There is a solidarity in the human Fall, both the man and the woman sinned; and (2) salvation is through faith alone in Jesus. But listen to this series of assertions. Paul is transparently clear here: Women are both to learn in quietness and to be silent. Is there any other way to say it? Paul thinks of a third way: "I do not permit a woman to teach or have authority over a man."

A woman should learn in quietness and full submission. I do not permit a woman to teach or have authority over a man; she must be silent. For Adam was formed first, then Eve. And Adam was not the one deceived; it was the woman who was deceived and became a sinner. But women will be kept safe [be saved] through childbirth, if they continue in faith, love and holiness with propriety.

1 Timothy 2:11–15

These teachings get full attention of the biblical interpreters. There are several attempts to resolve the problem. (1) Is this a specific teaching addressing a specific problem and not a universal rule?[6] (2) Is it a temporary "order" designed to keep the teaching channel open to prepared and wise teachers in an environment plagued by heresy and the abuse of ignorant teachers?[7] (3) Does the key to the passage lie in the unusual word translated "have authority over"?[8]

It is in looking at the word translated "have authority over" that the cryptic packages of strange teachings may at last make sense. The word *authentein* appears only here— nowhere else in the New Testament. Its translation appears to require the use of vulgar images. It is a term used in the secular culture from before New Testament times to as late as a letter from Clement of Alexandria. Its widespread use referred exclusively to the solicitation a prostitute uses in seducing a "customer" into sexual acts as a part of worship at the cult shrine. Far from any normal meaning of "teaching or having authority over," the language suggests "mixing religious teaching with sexual seduction." We would hope that Paul would put a stop to such a thing.

Yet exactly such things were what Clement of Alexandria was addressing. He deplored the fact that the communion service had, in some places, degenerated into a sex orgy. And two of the churches, Pergamum and Thyatyra, come in for denunciation because exactly the same encroachment of sexual seduction had contaminated them (Revelation 2:14, 18). The cryptic allusion to "accursed children" in the context of the indictment of "having eyes full of adultery" in 1 Peter 2:14, may provide powerful commentary on cracking this *authentein* passage in 1 Timothy. If these were converted but sexually addicted, ever-on-the-sexual-make, former prostitutes with their brood of illegitimate children, the whole text becomes illuminated.

Consider, too, the strange linkage of polarities in the teaching: "This is the will of God, even your sanctification, that you abstain from fornication" (1 Thessalonians 4:3). This microcosm of biblical teaching on personal holiness, linked as it is in polarity to the fornicating, instrumental, reductionistic exploitation of other people and the self, may serve us well. It is as if to say: You are either "hungering and thirsting after righteousness/sanctification/holiness" or you are on the roll in an endless and fruitless quest for satisfaction by competition, exploitation, and the instrumental use of people. St. Paul often uses polarity words to summarize enormous truth. "Be not drunk with wine, but be filled with the Spirit" again cautions that "You will be filled with some spirit! Beware lest it be a false and parasitic guest you take in! Get the 'real thing.'"

Should the linguistic analysis and historical-rhetorical study bear out this early interpretation based on the unique word *authentein*, then the passage might be focused toward a special, self-sorted, identifiable segment of the church: converted sexual addicts. It could then be interpreted to say: "I do not permit a woman to evangelize using sexual seduction; such must be silent . . . . But such women will be saved through faithfully rearing the children they have as they continue in faith, love, and holiness, with propriety."

So Paul may have taken off the gloves to address a painful, but persistent sexual problem in the early church, and one that continues to plague us. The connections between our sexuality and our spirituality are so complicated that patterns of past promiscuity tend to persist and to invade the spiritual domain unless explicit ground rules are followed. Paul seems to be offering some.

Silence! But Who?

We jump from *authentein* to what looks like a parallel teaching. Yet we are spared, here, from the string of children and from an Old Testament allusion. Here is straightforward, unmistakable language. If Paul wrote these words, he is either fickle or absent-minded and forgets that he has just outlined the specific ways a woman should comb her hair if she is going to speak or pray in public worship (chapter 11). It violates his baseline word on Christian initiation where there is neither Jew nor Greek, male nor female. Paul everywhere affirms women. He praises or applauds Dorcas, Lydia, and Priscilla for their part in spreading the gospel.

Is Paul schizophrenic, applauding women in one breath and then, in a single blow, forever silencing them in the church in another? Or does he? Because it is so contradictory of Paul's overall behavior and his basic teaching in his Epistles, many scholars regard this as part of a "soft" piece of text, likely not the work of Paul. "As in all the congregations of the saints, women should remain silent in the churches. They are not allowed to speak, but must be in submission, as the Law says. If they want to inquire about something, they should ask their own husbands at home; for it is disgraceful for a woman to speak in the church" (1 Corinthians 14:33–35). But now a handful of scholars, independent of each other, have discovered a repeated rhetorical pattern in 1 Corinthians. It strongly suggests that Paul quotes his enemies, mocks them, and uses the language of sarcasm. In his absence he may be using a caustic literary strategy in the letter.[9]

First, however, notice this: There is internal evidence that Paul is not using his typical vocabulary of Christian grace. "As in all the churches of the saints" seems to be a derisive label for the Judaizers from the Jerusalem community who are harassing his church planting, wanting everywhere to circumcise the men and to shut up the women. "As the Law says," is clearly a Judaistic allusion, not "as grace provides," a more typically Pauline kind of phrase. The role of women in this description is identical to that of the role of women in the Jewish synagogue: absolute silence; ask at home. But the rhetorical structure is also convincing:

A tiny Greek word, looking much like our letter "n," is an *eta*. It is pronounced "ay," much as Canadians punctuate their conversation with "eh?" Greek students today memorize an equivalent "or" and tend to bring it into English only in that way, or to ignore it altogether, as the New International Version repeatedly does. But the King James and Revised Standard Versions were more careful and also recognized "η" as a much more complicated conjunction than "or." Thayer's Greek-English Lexicon of the New Testament begins with a description of its unique service:

η, a disjunctive conjunction. Used to distinguish things or thoughts which either mutually exclude each other, or one of which can take the place of the other . . . . before a sentence contrary to the one just preceding, to indicate that if one be denied or refuted the other must stand . . . .

While the King James and the Revised Standard Versions translate the provocative "η" with "What!" or "What?" in many places, they, like the NIV, completely omit translating it in others. I am bringing together several places where Paul uses that conjunction. They appear at pivotal points in Paul's listing of shocking issues with which he must confront Corinth.

Remember, Paul is writing the 1 Corinthian letter in response to a report from Chloe's household (1:11) that serious divisions are splitting the church. If you look for the "η" in the Greek text, you may be seeing what made Paul see red. It appears that he quoted the Chloe "bill of particulars." He seems to introduce his attack in most cases by directly quoting the heresy as if to mockingly portray it as "truth." These Corinthian heresies then might be lifted out:

"I belong to Paul," "I belong to Apollos," "I belong to Cephas," "I belong to Christ" (1:12–14; 3:4).

"Every other sin which a man commits is outside the body; but the fornicator sins against his own body" (6:18).

"It is well for a man not to touch a woman" (7:1).

"Food will not commend us to God. We are no worse off if we do not eat, and no better off if we do" (8:8).

The "η" shows up in the Greek and often in the KJV "What!" or the RSV "What?" following these apparent Corinthian heresies. Wherever you see the "η," read "Nonsense!" and test the validity of the rhetorical argument:

If any of you has a dispute with another dare he take it before the ungodly for judgment instead of before the saints? [η] Do you not know that the saints will judge the world? . . . But instead, one brother goes to law against another—and this in front of unbelievers! . . . [η] Do you not know that the wicked will not inherit the kingdom of God? (6:1, 2, 9)

Do you not know that your bodies are members of Christ himself? Shall I then take the members of Christ and unite them with a prostitute? Never! [η] Do you not know that he who unites himself with a prostitute is one with her in body? For it is said, "The two will become one flesh." But he who unites himself with the Lord is one with him in spirit. (6:15–17)

All other sins a man commits are outside his body, but he who sins sexually [is a fornicator] sins against his own body. [η] Do you not know that your body is a temple of the Holy Spirit, who is in you, whom you have received from God? You are not your own; you were bought at a price. Therefore honor God with your body. (6:18–20)

Don't we have a right to take a believing wife along with us, as do the other apostles and the Lord's brothers and Cephas? [η] Is it only I and Barnabas who must work for a living? Who serves as a soldier at his own expense? Who plants a vineyard and does not eat of its grapes? [η] Who tends a flock and does not drink of the milk? Do I say this merely from a human point of view? [η] Doesn't the Law say the same thing? (9:5–8).

You cannot drink the cup of the Lord and the cup of demons too; you cannot have a part in both the Lord's table and the table of demons. [η] Are we trying to arouse the Lord's jealousy? Are we stronger than he? (10:21, 22).

Judge for yourselves: Is it proper for a woman to pray to God with her head uncovered? [η] Does not the very nature of things teach you that if a man has long hair, it is a disgrace to him, but that if a woman has long hair, it is her glory? For long hair is given to her as a covering. If anyone wants to be contentious about this, we have no other practice—nor do the churches of God. (11:13–16)

Finally, look at the passage in focus:

As in all the congregations of the saints, women should remain silent in the churches. They are not allowed to speak, but must be in submission, as the Law says. If they want to inquire about something, they should ask their own husbands at home; for it is disgraceful for a woman to speak in the church. [η] Did the word of God originate with you? [η] Are you the only people it has reached? If anybody thinks he is a prophet or spiritually gifted, let him acknowledge that what I am writing to you is the Lord's command. If he ignores this, he himself will be ignored.

1 Corinthians 14:33–38

Paul appears to be using the "pincer" argument. He states the popular heresy, then mocks it as if to say with "η," a sarcastic, "Nonsense!" Then he follows with the correction to the bad teaching. Here and in Chapter 11, Paul becomes quite exercised and calls the bluff on anyone who dares to perpetuate the nonsense he seeks to correct: "He himself will be ignored"!

Husbands as Chief Executive Officers of the Home?

We began our search for the meaning of "head" in Chapter 5, "'Head of the House': God's Order for Families?" We will look in depth at "head" as it describes the husband's relationship to the wife in Chapter 10, "'Head': Another Name for Husbands?" So here it will be enough simply to ask what image Paul and Peter may have had in mind when they used the term. A profound debate is presently under way among biblical scholars on the subject of the use of "head" by Paul.

In recent years, Stephen Bedale has been quoted widely in his assertion that "head" nowhere is used metaphorically to denote "authority over," but to denote "source" or headwaters from which the stream originates.[10] Now Wayne Grudem has marshalled a computer-based word search and has analyzed 2,336 examples of "head" in Greek literature, including the New Testament. He asserts that the word *kephale*, in which you can almost hear the English word "cephalic," nowhere may be translated "source," and in 16.2 percent of the "metaphoric uses" actually refers to "person of superior authority or rank," or "ruler," "ruling part."[11] But Fred Layman examines the 1 Corinthians 11 and Ephesians 5 passages and concludes that "headship" and "lordship" are not synonymous, accusing those who confuse the two of ignoring the text of Ephesians 5 where the woman's submission to the husband is "as unto the Lord," not to the husband in any literal sense. Layman further notes that the entire passage is focused on the radical change Christianity required in male behavior: mutual submission, reverence, and care, for their wives "as for their own bodies."[12]

Everyone agrees that the "head" language is metaphoric. That is, the word "head" is used to create an ordinary image to which we may liken a complicated, intangible reality. What is striking to us is that neither "source" nor "authority" is an immediate "image" that we would expect to evoke with the sound of "*kephale*/head." And where the word *soma* or "body" appears in the same context, the vacuum created by "head" cries out for the completing unitary image of wholeness. While Ridderbos agrees that there is implicit evidence suggesting the physiological metaphor, he regards it as untenable.[13]

We are not eager to abandon the positioning of such impressive scholars, but we must express an eagerness to urge a serious look at the nature of metaphors in any language. A metaphor consists of the use of a concrete, tangible reality widely known to hearers or readers which evokes an image which has obvious analogies to a more intangible, less well-known important reality. Let us ask you to look at the Ephesians five material with that metaphor definition in mind. We may expect that "head" and "body," should they appear, would "make sense" at the level of ordinary imaging by or dinary people:

. . . Submit yourselves to one another out of reverence for Christ.

Wives, submit to your husbands as to the Lord. For the husband is the HEAD of the wife as Christ is the HEAD of the church, his BODY, of which he is the Savior. Now as the church submits to Christ, so also wives should submit to their husbands in everything.

Husbands, love your wives, just as Christ loved the church and gave himself up for her to make her holy, cleansing her by the washing with water through the word, and to present her to himself as a radiant church, without stain or wrinkle or any other blemish, but holy and blameless. In this same way, husbands ought to love their wives as their own BODIES. He who loves his wife loves himself. After all, no one ever hated his own BODY, but he feeds and cares for it, just as Christ does the church—for we are members of his BODY. "For this reason a man will leave his father and mother and be united to his wife, and the two will become one flesh." This is a profound mystery—but I am talking about Christ and the church. However, each one of you also must love his wife as he loves himself, and the wife must respect her husband.

Ephesians 5:21–33

We have put HEAD and BODY in capital letters to illustrate the clear anatomical metaphors. Count them. Since the "*kephale*/head" metaphor appears along with a "*soma*/body" metaphor, we automatically "image" a wholistic unity. That image is synchonic, coordinated, and easily denotes health, productivity, and wholeness, every way.

Indeed, these are exactly the images that are evoked. Count them:

1. Husband is head.
2. Christ is head of the church, his body.
3. Heads love, wash, care for, and feed bodies.
4. Husbands do all of this for their wives, as bodies.
5. Christ does all of this for the church, his body.
6. All of this constitutes a profound mystery.

Now anyone with a flare for spotting metaphors and identifying the "growing edges of perception" which they infallibly represent, will be able to see that the metaphors begin bumping into each other in the Ephesians passage:

1. Husband is head of wife.
2. Christ is head of the church, his body.
3. Husbands love their own bodies, metaphor of their wives.
4. Christ loves the church, his body.
5. We are members of Christ's body.
6. Husbands and Christ care for and feed their bodies.
7. All of us are "body" in one sense or another.

If it is regrettable that Ridderbos finds the physiological analogy untenable, it is incredible that Grudem neglects even so much as to provide a category in his computer search in which to catalogue the obvious anatomical metaphor. He is so preoccupied with destroying the credibility of Bedale and the Mickelsons that he misses the trees for the forest. He marches right past his own evidence and is satisfied when he produces 16.2 percent of the metaphoric uses as "person of superior authority or rank" in contrast to 0 percent meaning "source or origin." Scholarship indeed must be wonderful.

Finally, consider what images come to mind if the simple anatomical image is allowed when you read the 1 Corinthians 11 statement on various heads: "Now I want you to realize that the head of every man is Christ, and the head of the woman is man, and the head of Christ is God" (1 Corinthians 11:3). For each, a "body" is evoked into existence. We then see:

1. Christ is the head of every man.
2. Man is the head of the woman.
3. God is the head of Christ.

Suddenly we see that the relationships and roles are mobile. Introduce a new person to a relationship and the role may be changed. Christ, for example, is both a head and a body. But so also is "man." The whole idea of "head" and "body" may prepare us for some surprises. Peter's Pentecost quotation of Joel suggested a return to some flexible, nontraditional roles. And a cryptic statement in Jeremiah 31 evokes yet another possibility: "Behold, the Lord will create a new thing on earth—a woman will protect a man."

In this chapter we have laid out all of the texts which seem to teach unilateral respect and inferior status for women. We have examined serious flaws and long-term, likely distortion of the interpretation, even the translation, of the ancient texts. But we have looked at the "other 99.9 percent of the biblical vision" to see that the main lines demand that we put these 22 verses into a perspective which attends to proportion and balance.

If there seem to be contradictions, we will know that the problem is ours—a human one. We may not have attended to all of the best data, we may be biased in the ways we look at texts, and none of us lives long enough to acquire experiential wisdom which could possibly be made to apply to all times and circumstances. Given those fragile and tentative realities, we are surely obligated to take seriously the Creation and the Redemption images in Jesus. We ourselves are so seriously impaired by living in a fallen world and living with interior booby traps which tend to make us blind to our own biases that we dare not pontificate finally from the base of our own experience or reason alone.

QUESTIONS PEOPLE ASK

Q: You have just opened up some Scripture passages in a way I never imagined possible. If your interpretation is right, why haven't the Bible scholars given us these teachings before?

A: Translating and interpreting Holy Scripture is both an art and a science. Every generation finds new work to do in analyzing and understanding the texts. So we are enjoying the accumulated skills and wisdom of several centuries of Bible scholarship. Perhaps the most serious handicap to understanding the Bible, whether you are a scholar or simply a devoted reader, is that we tend to impose our own biases and our own "worldview" to what we read. Just as no fish will ever discover water because it is the total, unreflected environment, so we tend not to be aware of the biases, the contaminants in which we live and move. Unfortunately, many Bible commentators and scholars were captive to a limited worldview and their own biases.

Add to all of these potential problems the fact that the Bible has been almost exclusively in the hands of males, and you have a possible insight into why texts dealing with women and with male-female relationships may have been seen "through the colored glasses" of the prevailing culture and attitudes toward women. But we are fortunate to have God's Word in our own language and in many translations. In general, the more recent translations tend to at least identify problems by citing footnotes or alternate readings.

8

Head and Body: The Complete Adam

△

We made an intentional visit to Washington D.C., our national capital, when our two sons were in first and fifth grades. After four days of saturation with the Smithsonian, the public national shrines and buildings, and the National Gallery of Art, we were all full. Mike, then about six years old, entertained us with his symptoms of overload. We heard amazing stories about "George Lincoln" and "Abraham Washington" for weeks afterward.

John and Mike wanted to rush through the National Gallery. But we were almost hypnotized by one room. We sat before a painting of *The Sacrament of the Last Supper* for more than an hour. The painting was not new to us, but its impressive size demanded verdicts that we evidently were not ready to make any time before. We read the program guide on the painting and were a little impatient. The symbolism was only slightly unfolded for us.

In the painting, Jesus, blond and transparent in the thoracic cavity, is seated at the center of a table facing us. His hands are gesturing toward himself and toward the ceiling. A glass of liquid stands on the table in front of Jesus. A

115

broken loaf of bread sits on the near edge of the table, the two halves a couple of feet apart. The heads of the twelve apostles are all bowed, rather extremely, so only the crowns of their heads are facing us. Behind the figure of Jesus is what appears to be an open window with strange "dodecahedron," a twelve-sided figure which the Greek Pythagoreans declared to be a symbol of the universe. Through the open window we are looking into the edge of an ocean or a bay, in which islands of singular gigantic rock formations rise in a semicircle which arches toward us as if to encircle us. The painting is executed with dominant colors of white and blue. We notice through the transparent torso of Jesus that a fishing boat is tethered to the shore. The boat is at about the exact point—in any opaque, two-dimensional examination of the piece—where the heart of Jesus would be if the transparent window through him showed the interior organs.

We notice suddenly that the heads of the apostles form an "arc" which if extended and closed, would include viewers who were up close to the painting. "Believers," we discover, form the tightest, most intimate, perhaps most protected of all relationships with Jesus. The rocky islands, we then notice, form yet another arc, which if extended to close a circle would take in a gigantic area: perhaps the world, the tangible physical planet for which Jesus died.

But suspended in air above the entire scene at the Supper table is a headless torso. The top edge of the picture frame, as if it were a guillotine, seems to have decapitated this body which is superimposed above everything—hanging between two worlds. Exactly. Here is the artist's image of the Body. It is Jesus' body, the church. It remains "in the world," while the Head has taken temporary leave. The church is the visible body, the head, Jesus Christ, is presently invisible to our senses of sight and sound. Now we do not see him, but the day will come when "every eye shall see his face."

In the painting, the arms, distended in an encompassing "open arms" posture characteristic of mothers everywhere, is striking an arc exactly parallel to that of the heads of the apostles. The viewers are drawn into the sacramental feast simply by taking the viewing position in the room. Salvadore Dali has made his point: The Body is Jesus continuing in the world through his apostolate: the Church. And the Body, the headless torso, remains, we may be sure, attached to the Head which is temporarily "out of the picture" and invisible to us.[1]

The Adam Body

In Chapter 2 we painted again the Creation images of the splitting of the original Adam. In *Bonding: Relationships in the Image of God*, we referred to the "Alpha Adam" who stands like the left end of a pair of bookends, the other one of which is Jesus: the Omega Adam.

Since Genesis two uses human anatomy as a metaphor by which to explain the complex relationships between man and woman, we will likely always miss the mark if we ignore the detail of the images there. Here as elsewhere, physiology too is a witness of the Creation. We will likely do ourselves more harm by mistrusting the apparent biology of the metaphor than by dismissing the Creation text as so metaphoric as to have little connection with the real world.

Eden becomes God's "operating room." The solitary Adam is no bachelor male. This "earthling" contains the only human "stuff" created by God. No new material is introduced. There is no second dip into "dust," no grafting from another linkage in the life chain outlined in the first chapter of Genesis.

The original Adam is stretched out for surgery. Here the images are impressive: God is the surgeon. Adam is the patient. The Lord God presides over the anesthesia. Adam's rib cage is opened. The divine Surgeon builds up the woman from the cellular material removed from Adam. The woman thus contains the same genetic code as in the original Adam. God presents the woman in mirror image to the residual Adam.

The original woman is the creative transformational clone of Adam. So clonelike is the woman that the residual, left-over parts, post-operative male describes her in identical twinlike terms:

> ". . . bone of my bones
> and flesh of my flesh;
> she shall be called 'Ishshah,'
> for she was taken out of 'Ish.'"

Creative geniuses who give us our space and biological fiction have not come close to matching this scenario.

Adam as Head and Body

We cannot miss the almost shadowlike central focus which goes immediately to the male and to the female. The male is a speaking mouth with high visual concentration on the female. The female is distinctly formed from cellular material from the body mass. It is easy, perhaps dangerous, to note some potential polarities which have emerged universally:

1. Males tend to score higher as "thinkers," women as "feelers."[2] Both use cognitive processes equally, but at a statistically significant rate, women are more likely to filter their reasoning through the concern for people and to weigh decisions on "the human impact."

2. Males tend to take an "objective" look-out tower view and to give advice, while females are more likely to take an empathetic, "subjective" perspective and listen. Women complain that their husbands, for example, cannot simply listen to them when they have had a bad day. The man typically wants to "fix it" by giving advice or even by taking direct action himself.[3]

3. Males tend to look out for, protect, and to deal with potential threats to their women by intercepting the invaders at a distance when their wives or families are in jeopardy. In contrast, females are more likely to spring into action to protect from a hovering, "defend to the death" stance of protection, most often engaging the "enemy" within the intimate turf of the nest. Then when the crisis is past, women tend to turn more often than men to behaviors which are explicitly those associated with nurturance and encompassing the threatened object of their concern, even when there is no presenting problem on which to focus their

care giving. The child or husband who has thus been "saved" often walks away grateful, but is unable to receive the abundant, affectionate care that is offered.

The un-split Adam offers us interesting material for speculation. Were the full spectrum of emotions all in place in one person? Was the "look-out-tower-see-them-and-stop-them" package of objective protection in place alongside of the more interior "unleash-the-full-force-of-emotional-energy-to-exterminate-the-foe" energies of subjective protection? Were "mind" and "heart" in dynamic but balanced tension? The reproductive question is irrelevant. Sexual differentiation was created explicitly because "it is not good that Adam should be alone," not for reproductive purposes.[4]

Now, what we see when we look at this male-female division of gifts and services is at least analogical if not made literal by the metaphor of the splitting of Adam. In Hebrew thought throughout the Old Testament, for example, the seat of emotions was believed to reside in the "bowels." And kidneys were given a special role for a higher function than filtering our body waste. "Heart" was less regarded as the seat of emotions than today, but was cited as the center for moral reasoning and choice. It would be easy to conclude that it is the Westernizing of humanity that has delivered everything into the brain. This reduces our conception of ourselves to that of a sort of top-heavy robot whose only significant operations occur in the "head."

But in Eden, when the "two became one flesh, naked and unashamed," we see the image of wholeness, and specifically of a primeval holiness and mutuality by which the unique, newly differentiated powers also formed "one whole person." "Headship" and "bodyship" in Eden were clearly designed to look like something much better than General Motors Corporation vs. the United Auto Workers union.

Two as One: The Mystery of Complementarity

In Eden the "two as one" denotes forever the ideal of full complementarity. There is no suggestion that either ought to become like the other. But there is the clearest of all possible messages that it is their differences which fill in their mutual deficits, yielding the stunning portrayal of full and complete humanity.

The "reunion" of the sexually differentiated partners is specifically at the unique point of that differentiation: their sexuality. Identity in each of us is so deeply connected with our sexuality that the giving and uniting with another person at the genital level denotes the ultimate, final surrender of the self to the other. It should not be surprising to us that the linkage between identifiable blood type is matched by identical images visible in analysis of reproductive material. Nor should it be surprising that the most deadly of the sexually transmitted diseases move within the intimate body fluids into the lifestream of the partner.

It is by the gesture of "one flesh" intimacy that lovers are granted the franchise to participate in creation. Their child becomes the "one flesh" gift which forever denotes the reality of their union. But the gestures of loving which unite two persons sexually leaves the intangible bond by which they know as if instinctually that they have "become one flesh." The bonding is present in young lovers or old. Only the sexual addict, the promiscuous person, has suffered the "hardening of the bonding" sensitivity. Persons have become objects. But that tragic story is unfolded in *Re-Bonding: Preventing and Restoring Broken Relationships*.

When the bonding attraction of "opposites" is healthy and when the two lovers are nicely settled in ego development and wholeness, you will see them each tending to the business they do best. As if by reflex, the male is inclined to be the protector and problem-solver. It is almost as if he cannot *not* fill those roles. And the female is similarly inclined to look after her husband's more interior needs, often invisible to people who do not know him well. St. Paul notes these two polarities in his famous description of how each submits to the other in Ephesians 5 and 6. There the wife submits to the husband as "head," just as the church honors Jesus as its "head." But the husband lays down his life to protect the wife, loving her "as he loves his own body." The anatomic metaphor is complete. Body and head form a unity. They are one, and while their instinctual, Creation-gifted motivations to serve each other differ toward their unique polarities, they are mutually interdependent as the head and the body unit is in which each of us lives and moves and has our being on this planet.

So watch for the wonder when the mystery of sexual bonding is under way. You will see it on the faces of both younger and older lovers, and you will know that it denotes the attraction of opposites who, together, form "one flesh."

Servanthood as Submission and Synchronicity: The Dance of Marriage

Here we confront a basic principle which undergirds both the Creation gift of our mutually dependent sexuality, and which must also form the foundation for our continuing relationship in marriage. We will not be surprised that the marital principle also forms a microcosm from which we can infer to all other human relationships, and that the family system is the primary rehearsal and formation arena for our participation in larger social and political systems.

The principle is this: Whole persons form mutually interdependent relationships with those whose gifts differ from their own. They enter into those relationships noncompetitively but with reverence. They participate in the relationships spontaneously, almost naïvely, assuming that they enjoy the same equitable acceptance and respect which they extend to the other. Whole persons may be observed both to listen and to initiate. They can debate without name-calling or put-downs. And when the best has been offered all around, they can consolidate, contribute to decisions, and eagerly implement what the consensus has produced, owning it without clinging to an individualistic, peevish, personal perspective they refuse to modify.

In this chapter we have looked at the "Head" and "Body" metaphors straight out of anatomy. And we cannot escape seeing the futility of adversary struggles over power. We see, every morning in the mirror, the image which Scripture has held up to us: the absolute necessity for each part of the human anatomy to be cared for so as to assure that it serves all other parts well. "Love your spouse as you love your own body" is a call for celebrating the unity, the collegiality, and the synchronism of marriage. Any preoccupation with any other use of "head" should quickly wither under the judgment of the central imagery from Eden until now.

QUESTIONS PEOPLE ASK

Q: *You make me a little nervous with all of this "biology" mixed in with theology. Are you buying into "biological determinism"?*

A: Biological determinism would hold that the anatomy and the biological system "control" all of life. That is precisely what we reject. But we reject, too, the idea that anyone can "get theology straight in the head" and ignore the biological evidences of God's Creation. For this reason we speak often of the "three witnesses which must ultimately come into agreement: Creation, Scripture, and Jesus. We reject determinism of all kinds, including that which might claim to be rooted in any one of the three witnesses while ignoring the others. We are always eager to hold out the troublesome questions and the puzzles of real life and summon the witnesses to speak. We are especially eager to identify any harmonious way that biology, theology, and faith may unite to enrich us all.

9

Jesus Has a Plan for Families

△

Sitting there in the gigantic men's Bible study on a Tuesday evening at Lovers' Lane United Methodist Church in Dallas, I was suddenly in theological shock. I'm afraid I took an introvert's jet plane and left the innocent and gentle Exxon executive who was expounding "God's order for families" from the tragic text in the Book of Esther. I had my Bible in my lap. There it was, all in the first chapter of Esther, and suddenly I was seeing minor points in the story that I had missed in my marathon readings of the Old Testament. The story took on new dimensions.[1] This expositor was unafraid to treat tragic, heathen passages as "normative" for the godly home. That had never occurred to me as even a possibility.

What, indeed, was the context for the "vertical marriage" decree by King Xerxes? It was embarrassing:

1. The king had thrown an "open house" for six months— 180 days. "The military leaders of Persia and Media, the princes, and the nobles of the provinces were present."

2. The climax of the six-month party was an intensive week-long banquet, ". . . lasting seven days, in the enclosed garden of the king's palace, for all the people from the least to the greatest . . . ."

3. They were saturated with liquors suited to the taste of every guest: "By the king's command each guest was allowed to drink in his own way, for the king instructed all the wine stewards to serve each man what he wished."

4. Queen Vashti was holding a parallel banquet for the women in the royal palace, as well.

5. "On the seventh day, when King Xerxes was in high spirits from wine, he commanded the seven eunuchs who served . . . to bring before him Queen Vashti, wearing her royal crown, in order to display her beauty to the people and nobles, for she was lovely to look at."

6. The Queen refused—for reasons not stated, but implied: the king was regarding her as an instrument, an object, and was arbitrarily commanding her appearance for purposes of his own status, but at the expense of her becoming the sex target of the invited and now drunken guests.

7. "The king became furious and burned with anger."

8. The legal question immediately was raised by Memucan: "Queen Vashti has done wrong, not only against the king but also against all the nobles and the people of all the provinces of King Xerxes. For the queen's conduct will become known to all the women, and so they will despise their husbands . . . This very day the Persian and Median women of the nobility who have heard about the queen's conduct will respond to all the king's nobles in the same way. There will be no end of disrespect and discord."

9. So the decree was written "in the laws of Persia and Media, which cannot be repealed." The law thus banished Vashti from her marriage and her office as queen. "Then when the king's edict is proclaimed throughout all of his vast realm, all the women will respect their husbands, from the least to the greatest."

10. The "post office" bulletins were dispatched throughout the realm, well ahead of the return of the dignitaries to their provinces: "Every man should be ruler over his own womenfolk."

I could see why the Exxon lecturer was mildly apologetic for citing the passage as an authoritative teaching about marriage relationships. I wondered, but only silently and

inwardly, what position the lecturer might have taken if
someone had asked whether it was right that Esther was
about to marry this drunken bum of a legally divorced king.
But I knew he would pull back from such an inconvenient use
of the story. To this day, it is a "divorce/remarriage issue"
I have never heard addressed in the Queen Esther story. I
was being cynical, but my introspective, computerlike analysis and reflection suddenly exploded the key question which
I knew I had to answer. I was now in search of a dis-
tinctively Christian model of the family for today:

Does Jesus Have a Word?

Surely, I thought, *there must be a clear teaching from
Jesus that would throw light on this kind of abuse of power,
this arbitrary assumption that husbands can use wives, employers can use employees, and one social class can exploit
another.* I asked myself, "What is the word from Jesus?"
Before our car had made the trip from the Love Field
area of Dallas into the heart of Arlington, I knew my mental
computer had found the answer. I suspect now, nearly ten
years later, that I might never have connected the principles
of Jesus to the power model of marriage if I had not been
invited to that men's Bible study group one spring night in
Dallas. Here is the NIV rendering of the words of Jesus
recorded in Matthew 20:

> You know that the rulers of the Gentiles love to lord it over
> them [the Gentiles], and their high officials exercise authority
> over them [the rulers]. Not so with you. Instead, whoever
> wants to become great among you must be your servant, and
> whoever wants to be first among you must be your slave—just
> as the Son of Man did not come to be served, but to serve, and
> to give his life as a ransom for many.[2]

A more shocking paraphrase is Ken Taylor's *Living Bible:*

> Among the heathen, kings are tyrants, and each minor official
> loves to lord it over those beneath him. But among you it is
> quite different.

In a single, sweeping teaching, Jesus disconnects the redeemed person from traditional, power-based ways of relating to people. And he does it in a way that applies to every human relationship, including marriage.

These days it is quite common to hear teachings on "servanthood." Regrettably, many who teach it apply it only to evangelism or Christian social responsibility in the world outside the home. The idea of a "servant" marriage often seems never to have occurred to those of us males who have been captivated by servanthood as a model for ministry. "Servant," it turns out, is Jesus' word which is the equivalent of St. Paul's "submission." And submission is a concept which tends to be taught most stridently and almost exclusively by those of us who wish to invoke it as the requirement for women who are, by definition, then, "beneath us," to use Ken Taylor's "heathen" language from Matthew 20.

At What Price the Vertical Marriage and Family?

Look at the context for Jesus' teaching about "servant relationships," as an alternative to power-brokering our way to success:

1. The "mother of Zebedee's sons [a fallen, power-oriented social order that regarded the woman and the children as the property of the man] came to Jesus with her sons and, kneeling down [the posture of devalued self-esteem while 'paying one's dues' or when in the presence of a perceived power source], asked a favor of him ['Beg of you Mr. Charlie, suh?']."

2. "Grant that one of these two sons of mine may sit at your right and the other at your left in your kingdom," she requested.

3. When Jesus asked whether they were able to drink of the cup he would have to drink, they responded either naïvely or arrogantly, "We are able." A famous song echoes the line, but ignores the embarrassing context.

4. Jesus assures them that suffering with him "comes with the territory," but "to sit at my right or left is not for me to grant. . . ."

5. The eavesdropping ten "were indignant with the two brothers." That power-centered event evoked the succinct and radically Creation-based statement of a principle about human relationships and the use of power.

Consider the high price of verticalizing any relationship from marriage to your secular organization:

The heathen model feeds pride. Watch the next "search committee" process at your favorite institution or organization. When the race horses have been trotted around the viewing arena and the winner announced, there is a "winner." The others are not winners, but have set up the horse race situation which will forever separate them from the person who may have been a true colleague and peer before the "search" separated them by verticalizing the value of persons into winners or losers.

We worked for many years with a Christian statesman who wanted all conversations to be informal and exploratory, until the person had been found who was obviously the only one for the open slot. At first we regarded it as devious, especially when he prepared a group of us to host one particular guest at a series of meals. But then his final line to us was a profound disclosure: "Our guest has an enormously fine reputation, and if he is disqualified from joining us on some nonnegotiable fine point, it must never be said that he interviewed for this job and was turned down. You are the evaluation team, but he is not an official candidate. Do you have any questions?" We were stunned but had no questions. The person was more important than institutional protocol or pride.

The heathen model with its "win-lose" competition breeds hostility. The ten disciples were provoked to jealousy by the thought that two of their number were principals in a power play. Most of us are still vulnerable to the "racers' edge" impulse. We show it in the way we drive, the way we negotiate stop lights, and by our addictions to competition as innocent as the soccer field or the basketball court. If you want to see the "dip stick" measure on original sin, just watch a group of seminarians play basketball! If bishoprics are won competitively, you might be able to crystal-ball the future ecclesiastical power-brokers in a few minutes of analytical watching.

The heathen model exploits persons. It is inevitable that the people "down the ladder" in the chain of command get used. Whether it is a marriage, an official church board, or a corporation, power-brokers use the people they control. There are reports to be written, menial, time-consuming tasks to be done, and the "job description" details "any other tasks as delegated by the supervisor." And in the truly heathen model, the assignments are (1) arbitrary, (b) urgently needed at once, (c) without appropriate compensation, and (d) to be "ghost written" so as to "make the boss look good," as if the boss had completed the work single-handedly.

The exploitation may be more subtle. Even our use of titles sometimes suggests who the second class citizens are. "Diaconal ministers" in one major denomination are primarily so labeled to distinguish them from other ministry career people who have full vote and full perks: parsonages, full insurance coverages, and so forth.

One pastor illustrated the hazards of status by rank when he reported how his congregation had wrestled with pastoral titles. There was an extended debate over whether the second full-time staff member would be designated "Associate Pastor" or "Assistant Pastor." Then someone observed that it didn't make much difference, since the abbreviation for both would be the same. Titles in themselves tend to be denoting either exaltation or exploitation. So the congregation determined to refer to all ministry staff by one title: Pastor. Their reasoning was compelling. The service given would earn the honor and status appropriate to the community's life; titles could never guarantee either. To attempt to discriminate by a horse race or by layered titles is to play out the heathen tendencies we all have. While it appears to build a sense of high self-esteem among the winners, it produces another effect:

The heathen model wastes resources. Many years ago we were present when a supervisor quieted a woman driver who offered a suggestion about how to improve the effectiveness of the rather complicated corporate operation:

"I am not paying you to think, I am paying you to drive a truck." And he proceeded with his rehearsal of complaints about what had gone wrong during the last few hours.

The more benevolent monarchs invite "suggestions" from their underlings, often paying rewards for ideas for improving the profit position of the company. Sometimes they are made "employee of the week." But today the major corporations are experimenting with "theory z" in an effort to find a way to conserve all of the resources of all of the people.

In a marriage, when either partner is "silenced," the losses in perspective, resources, and imagination are staggering. Heathen competitive management not only deploys the chief executive officer to an absurdly lonely position, sitting atop the totem pole; the lonely executive is also deprived of the richness of basic information and dialogue which might have made the ship at least unsinkable if not arrogantly omniscient.

In vertical marriages everyone loses. The silenced spouse retreats to the world within, populated as it may be with a spectrum that ranges from rage to indifference with its resulting atrophy and waste. The domineering spouse is perpetually in the position of having to make all decisions, take responsibility for any flaws that develop, possess all intelligence, and do all of it instantly.

In 1974, we were mellowed right down by the wedding vows that showed up in the Julie Cutler–John Joy wedding. They had forged them in poetic lines and dropped them in the middle of a quite traditional liturgy. The vows were adapted from Kahlil Gibran's *The Prophet.*[3]

> I feel as if we were born together, and will
>   be together forever.
> We will be together when the white wings of death
>   shall scatter our days.
> And we will still be together in the arms of God.
>
> I will love you, but will not make a bondage of love.
> Let us make our love into a moving sea
>   between the shores of our souls.
> Let us sing and dance together and be joyous,
>   but let us each remain ourselves.
> Even as the strings of a lute are alone
>   though they quiver with the same music.

Let us stand together,
    yet not too near together.
Let us remember that the pillars of the temple
    stand apart,
And the oak tree and the cypress grow together,
    but not in each others' shadow.

In the years that have followed we have watched. On the tenth anniversary there was a "backyard re-marriage" complete with new vows of tenderness which reflected the winepress of life's trouble, all executed in the eyes of an eight-year-old "best man," a five-year-old bridesmaid, and a three-year-old ring bearer—their children. "One of the best things about our marriage," that couple reports, "is that neither of us has to be always right or always strong or always first or always smart, but between the two of us we find that we can handle almost anything."

The heathen model is explicitly condemned by Jesus. Perhaps that is enough. But Jesus was not one to be arbitrary. He knew much more than we have described here about how ineffective the heathen/power model is in marriages, families, churches, and industry.

The late Dr. Gilbert James once delivered a campus lecture whose main focus was this: the central tendency of all institutions is toward the demonic—toward the abuses characteristic of "principalities and powers." A few months later at a ministers' training event in the Detroit area he closed the conference, sharing the platform with a denominational executive whose "organizational chart" from his plenary session was still nearby on the platform. As a moderator fielded the questions from conference participants, one was directed to Dr. James. "What would you suggest for our denomination and its organizational structure, since you said that all institutions have a central tendency toward becoming demonic and power machines?"

Gilbert James, it is reported, rose from the table where he was seated with the other guest. He moved toward the easel and the organizational chart. Then, grasping it top and bottom, he flipped the chart one hundred and eighty degrees— upside down. Then, walking back to his seat he said, "I think that would be a good place to start." Exactly. Jesus said the same thing. Let us regard ordination as the "lowest order." The only lower position would be that of area supervisor or bishop. Just as a tree delivers its fruit on the network of complex branches where the light and sun mix, so also the tree draws its resources up from below where the servant roots do their hidden, supportive, nurturing work.

What Kind of Chain for Decision-Making?

Wherever there are people in pairs or groups, some game plan will have to be worked out to distribute the responsibilities and to check on what happens to strategic jobs that have to be done. If the vertical chain of command

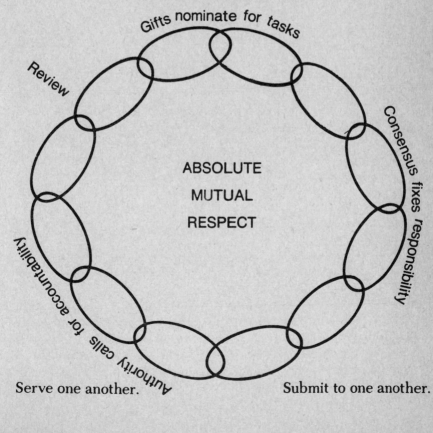

A Servant-Submission Chain

Gifts nominate for tasks

Review

Consensus fixes responsibility

ABSOLUTE
MUTUAL
RESPECT

Authority calls for accountability

Serve one another.   Submit to one another.

is condemned by Jesus, flat out, then how are those responsibilities and accountabilities to be handled? Here are some structures and strategies we have worked through:

1. Gifts, not gender or seniority, nominate for responsibility.

2. Consensus, sometimes with trial periods for experimentation, fix responsibility.

3. Authority goes with the assignment, and implies regular feedback and accountability.

4. Evaluation and review is also by consensus and may lead to a redistribution of responsibility to better match gifts, now based on experience and review.

The structures and strategies will not work unless they are supported by:

5. Absolute mutual respect.

6. Consistent mutual submission.

Who Makes Final Decisions?

In any organization or ongoing set of relationships, there are obvious responsibilities which "go with the turf." Where authority has been fixed by consensus, that is, by mutual agreement, it is clear that the responsibilities to make decisions belong to that person. In the most complex organization, even a heathen one, a chief executive officer could not possibly make all of the decisions. It is inconceivable that any committee of two—a marriage—would elect officers. Some guidelines for determining who makes final decisions might look like this:

1. The person to whom responsibility and authority has been assigned.

2. By corporate consensus if the decision is regarded as too complex or far-reaching for any one person acting independently.

3. If there is no consensus, make no decision.[4]

When people respect each other, they will not demand a quick decision or take things into their own hands to satisfy their appetite for instant gratification. This effective "veto power" cannot be used as manipulation in a marriage or a corporation without reaping a harvest of blame and guilt.

But mutual respect and mutual submission always means, "If you cannot get the consent of your mind or heart just now, the decision can wait." And in a marriage, that statement carries another deeper message: "You are more important to me than having what I want right now."

Mirror, Mirror on the Wall, Who Is the Powermonger?

It is the nature of egocentrism and of the original sin that our deepest motivations sometimes remain hidden to us. One effort to study motivation for moral action is a research field called by at least two names. One is "moral development" or "moral reasoning." The other is "structuralism." One of the more fascinating discoveries is that healthy ego strength is characterized by a unique attribute. The person who must make a choice does so prepared to exchange places with any of the people affected by the decision. This personal quality is called "perspectivism: the ability to see things from multiple points of view."

Most of us need mentors, confidential moral and spiritual "directors" or other care givers to whom we can say, "Let me tell you what I am feeling, or what I am about to do. Ask me everything that comes to mind. I do not trust myself to be objective in this whole thing."

Scott Peck has given us a first draft psychiatric definition of "evil." It may be all the more compelling because Dr. Peck comes to the writing of *People of the Lie* without a significant theological background, only recently announcing that he has received Christian baptism. Peck describes clinical evil this way:

a. Consistent destructive, scapegoating behavior, which may often be quite subtle.
b. Excessive, albeit usually covert, intolerance to criticism and other forms of narcissistic injury.
c. Pronounced concern with a public image and self-image of respectability, contributing to a stability of lifestyle but also to pretentiousness and denial of hateful feelings or vengeful motives.

    d. Intellectual deviousness, with an increased likelihood
of a mild schizophreniclike disturbance of thinking at
times of stress.[5]

Peck offers a caution to those of us who live and move in the
glow of a specifically, self-avowed religious lifestyle. "We
come now to a sort of paradox," Peck writes. "I have said
that evil people feel themselves to be perfect. At the same
time, however, I think they have an unacknowledged sense
of their own evil nature. Indeed, it is this very sense from
which they are frantically trying to flee."[6] He suggests that
we learn to detect the reality of evil by the smoothness of its
disguise. Since the primary motive of evil is disguise, one of
the most likely places to find evil people of high ambition is
in the church. Where better to hide? he asks.

Perhaps the question at the Last Supper is not merely
rhetorical. "Lord, is it I?" is always appropriate. "Show me
my heart; I am too embroiled in the whole tangle of life to
know my own motivation."

In almost direct contrast to Peck's psychiatric definition
of evil are the conclusions of faith development researcher,
Dr. James W. Fowler of Emory University. In describing
adult Christian maturity he asserts that such a "vocation" is
a call "to personhood in relationships. There is no personal
fulfillment that is not part of a communal fulfillment. We
find ourselves by giving ourselves. . . . Christians see our
potential as humans to be represented, as it says in Ephesians
4:13, 'in a mature personhood that partakes of the measure
of the stature which belongs to the fullness of Jesus Christ.'"
Fowler identifies specific characteristics of Christian maturity in stark contrast to Peck's "evil" domain:

    a. Devoted to excellence without competition.
    b. Freedom—beyond jealousy—to rejoice in all excel-
lence, the gifts and graces of others.
    c. Freedom to do our work, pursue our destiny, finding
myriad ways to join God's activity.
    d. Freedom from having to please everybody.
    e. Called to seek and maintain a responsible balance in
the investment of our time and energy.

f. Sees time as a gift, therefore life and death are only markers, boundaries on the gift.

g. Sees the human and Christian vocation, ever refining, ever changing its focus.[7]

In this chapter, we have wanted you to discover Jesus' word on relationships. We have wanted you to put popular teachings about the chain of command into the perspective of both Creation and Gospel. We then wanted you to explore a set of guidelines for living out the Jesus-way of leading by "service" and submission. We have more work to do on the biblical teachings, but we have a clear word from Matthew 20 governing all of our relationships.

All of this, perhaps, leaves us with the dream of what every marriage might be. Only two years ago, brooding over some of these issues, we developed a statement of what we imagine is a universal human dream:

The marriage we long for is one in which
>together we can be sure
>of the best decisions,
>the fullest set of options,
>the most balanced perspective,
>the best-resourced effort.

Such a marriage means absolute
>trust,
>honesty,
>integrity,
>and mutual respect.

It means that neither of us alone is
>always right,
>always strong,
>always the leader, or
>always the follower.

But together we can face anything.

QUESTIONS PEOPLE ASK

Q: I've always felt responsible for making decisions for my family. How can I go about helping my wife and children become responsible for part of our decisions?

A: Bravo! Everyone will thank you for bringing everyone "on line" in responsibility. Teachers and future employers of your children will praise you when they see good self-control, excellent work habits, and readiness to take responsibility for what happens, whether it turned out well or badly. At our house we make lists of things that need to be done, then we decide who is closest to the item and whether they have the gifts and motivation to handle it entirely by themselves. If they do, they get the nod to carry through. And children deserve to have daily or weekly "work lists" of their responsibilities. Few of us need penalties if we fail to work through our lists; just seeing the items in a conspicuous but private location is often all we need to "get with it."

Q: *Isn't "final responsibility" too strong a word to use for a woman's or a child's carrying out their assigned tasks?*
A: It would be if the husband and father was a "chief executive officer of the corporation," as many people suggest he should be. When he is "president," then he himself is responsible for everything else. He "delegates" the authority and responsibility, but if the person fails, then it becomes his responsibility for making a bad delegation or assignment as well as for doing the work himself. This works efficiently for managing corporations, but not even effectively there. And it is deadly in the family. In the first place the husband and father must carry the full load of all responsibilities. But the more tragic loss is in keeping wife and children forever "dependent," prevented from becoming truly and fully human. If the home is a "school" for preparation to make adult decisions, then absolute final authority must be given, with enough room for both good and poor decisions to be made and the consequences brought right back to the person who had the full responsibility for making those decisions.

Q: *I like your picture and explanation of the "circular chain" of family responsibilities. But how would it work, exactly?*
A: First of all, this kind of dynamic in a family requires a lot of "listening." It moves on asking questions instead of short circuiting conversation to shut down the participants.

Mutual respect is going to take a little more time, a lot more courtesy, but the rewards are unbelievable.

Let's take the toughest case—that of a young child of early school age. Does that youngster have anything to contribute to the family? Well, not a whole lot. But the child has preferences when it comes to where to eat on a special day out, and what television shows to watch. Let's stress that the family needs to use mealtimes and other more structured gatherings to list an agenda of things that need to be done and must be decided. When the question "Who will do it?" arrives, the six-year-old candidate may be very well qualified and also quite willing. If it involves phoning to invite guests to a party, or setting up the back yard for a picnic, the person who is "in charge" needs to be set free to do it without constant meddling supervision which effectively strips away the assignment. Yet in "chain of command" households you will find that anybody can criticize, cancel, or otherwise harass anyone "beneath" them until they cannot develop responsibility that leads to accountability at the end of the task. Accountability goes with the territory of "responsibility," but it has due time to complete the task before being evaluated.

Q: But doesn't somebody have to have final responsibility for making a decision? Isn't that the man's place?

A: Try consensus. Whenever a committee of two has to "vote" on an issue, it is a power politics maneuver and it reveals that competition, not cooperation, is the driver. Within the family, it is critical to bring everybody along and to give time for consensus to form. We learned an enormous lesson years ago when the Aldersgate Graded Curriculum Project was being launched. Serious conflict emerged as we were hammering out some of the "foundation values" that the cooperating denominational leaders had to write. It was two Quaker women at the table, representing the Evangelical Friends Alliance, who asked quietly at the end of a painful and almost abortive session, "Have you ever thought of making decisions by consensus instead of by vote? We do it that way in the Meeting." Faced with the option the next morning, there was agreement to try consensus. Suddenly the climate changed. Now, instead of "position speeches," it became necessary to listen! We took no more votes in the entire history of the project, concluding that anything on which we could not reach consensus did not have to be decided now. And in a family, "forced decisions" which overpower objections often come at a very high price and are more a symptom of pride and arrogance than of "final responsibility." Try it.

10

"Head": Another Name for Husbands?

△

Paul Brand, surgeon among the lepers of India for a full missionary career, has shared with us in two books many of the theological insights that came to him from his daily encounters with physiology and surgery. Surely among the most powerful of his "theological analogies" is that having to do with the human head.[1]

Dr. Brand reports that two years of medical school had not prepared him for the day he was given his own cadaver head. He had chosen to trace the nerves from each of the "sensors" into the brain—from the tongue, eyes, ears, and nose. He needed to expose the nerve patterns to trace the pathways himself.

"What is the appropriate way to transport a cadaver head?" was his first unexpected problem. "Hold it by the ears? Grasp the scalp as you would pick up a kitten?" Textbooks, he says, had never mentioned such things.

Brand tells us that seeing inside the human head is a revolutionary experience. "A whole person lies inside the bony box, locked in, protected, sealed away for the indispensable duties of managing one hundred trillion cells in a human

139

body." He likens Jesus' departure from the infant church as the historical moment when his mission was "confined" into the Head so as to unite with the Body, the church, newly created, as one symphonic whole.

The brain, that principal deposit in the human head, Brand points out, never "sees" in a literal sense. "If I opened one up to light, I would likely harm it irreparably." Nor does the brain "hear," but it is so cushioned that it only transforms reverberating sensations into the finest discriminations of sound. Nor does the brain experience any sense of "touch." Indeed, it has no feelings of its own, and may undergo surgical procedures without anesthesia. But the brain is able to process touch sensations from the entire body and instantly to decode the sensations so as infallibly to note the exact location of the pain, the tickling, or the burn.

And while the cells of every human body undergo constant change, replacing themselves at least every seven years, yet the brain and nerve cells remain. They are always the same, the original equipment. And in these permanent cells the identity of every person remains constant.

What a Head Does Best

There it is. In those metaphors of a marriage or of the church which use "head" and "body," the physiological analogy is explicit and inescapable. Look at the role of the head in the "head-body" image:

The location of the head at the top of the body denotes less of its "authority" than of its "utility." The periscope, the head locates trouble, scouts maximum terrain, and thus cares for the safety of the entire person. From this high look-out point the sensory receptors sort out options. With these evaluated, the resources of the head enable the feet, legs, and torso to tilt and change direction to match decisions made on the basis of what is seen, smelled, or heard.

Indeed, the coordination of the entire body mass is a gift from the head. The central nervous system, rooted as it is in the brain, brings the entire person into a synchronized and fully harmonious pattern of behavior. There are no "disagreements" between body and head, since all messages of the body are being analyzed so effectively that "decisions" made in the head are never handed down in ways that ignore the body's signals. Hunger pangs, for example, are encoded from signals in the digestive system. But those hunger pangs are decoded and interpreted in the head. The urgent demand of the excretory system, similarly, is encoded in messages signalled from the sigmoid colon. But the decision to find the next "comfort station" or "rest stop" is made in the head. If physiology mirrors organizational structures, the message is overwhelming: Head and body are one! Any adversary positioning would be absurd. And any effort to contradict signals of the body by decisions of the head only postpones and complicates the urgent issues. There will be the devil to pay if the basic body messages are overruled for long.

The head is the "identity" point of the total person. It features the "face" which we associate with the "person." In naming the person, it is common to name the face, to focus on the head. Here a one-tenth denotes the whole! Change bodies and two people might escape detection for the fraud, the weight of identification goes with an inappropriately small proportion of the whole person.

The head is the entry point for nourishment. Should toxic food be engorged, it is the whole person who suffers, but it is the body which must go into action to expel the poison. Sometimes the body can bear the burden with its digestive processes, but occasionally the mistake must make its exit through the head.

The head articulates. By encoding into language and other socially recognized forms of communication, the head negotiates relationships with the outer world. But if bound and gagged or if speech or hearing dysfunction is present, the body may take over with crude or sophisticated "hand speech." "Body language" is always the stereophonic second track which verifies or contradicts the speech coming from the mouth.

The head is vulnerable. A blow to the head can immobilize the entire person. "Head wounds are mortal" is both physiology and theology, as the serpent learned in Genesis three. So the body instinctually springs to defend the head—to throw up arms, to "duck" the head below the normal periscope level, even to capsize the head in the event of possible major catastrophe, letting the body take the major impact of a fall or a crash.

The head is naked. It is so fully active in the tasks which fall to it, that except where the hair is meant to be, no part may be covered, or clothed, without impairing safety. It is exposed in severe weather of all kinds, doing, as it must, its "periscope" work, about which it never complains.

What a Head Needs Most

While a head might crank out ideas, programs, or decisions, none of them will ever come into existence and reality without the action that involves the body. If anyone wanted to find a metaphor denoting "mutuality," it would be hard to improve on the "head-body" image. When hunger strikes, it is the hands which must both prepare and "feed" the food to the head.

The body makes up about ninety percent of the person's tangible substances. The complicated skeleton, muscles, and vital organ structures pale beside the complexity of the brain. But in the body all of this mysterious self-maintaining ecosystem is at work, indeed a mystery of creative ingenuity.

The body's operations to support life outnumber those of the head by about three to one. Some are "paired," like lungs and kidneys, so that one of the pair might be lost without jeopardizing life itself. But life ends with loss of heart, liver, or digestive system. The same is true, obviously, of the head, and it is not "paired." But an assassin more often attempts to strike a vital point in the upper torso than to hit the relatively smaller, moving head.

The body supports the head. Think of the body as the "frame" for the picture of the person: the head. Or think of the body as the piece of jewelry which exhibits the jewel: the head. In all of these, there is a certain elegance of proportion, balance, symmetry, and configuration. But the body is the "foundation," the absolute sure footing for the rather awkward, globelike top appendage: the head. Watch a child of twelve or thirteen months try to negotiate first steps or to sit upright. The body and head weights are so nearly balanced that there will be occasional "upsets," as the body crashes down. The body is still undeveloped and lacks the stabilizing weight and substance to anchor the head.

The body is both the "gatherer" and the "distributor" when compared to the "observer-decider" role of the head. But the head goes with the body into the marketplace, the restaurant, or the chapel. Indeed the "workhorse," the body goes all day long at the most taxing pace, exerting full energy. Eventually its signals all say "quit," and the head which has been taking a free ride all day agrees and provides the signals for sleep.

The body carries out its synchronized basic operations quietly, unobtrusively. The body does its work without calling attention to its importance. Besides its silence, the body tends to be hidden away behind the "blind" of clothing. Yet let respiration, digestion, or circulation fall on bad times, and the "vital signs" are put in jeopardy. The health of the person depends on the maintenance of the workhorses of the organism—in the body.

Reproduction occurs in the body. Here the conceiving, life-engendering miracle occurs. Here the new life is formed and from the body it is launched. The new person is umbilically attached from body to body, not from head to head. Perhaps "individuality" requires this "body-to-body" launching, lest the parental "image" would be overpowering and would prevent the new life from having an autonomous existence of its own.

Can you imagine a head without a body? Or a body without a head? It has been an absurd sort of analysis to examine some of the things heads and bodies do, but the New Testament language about *kephale* and *soma* invite us to get our pictures straight.

Watch a Head at Work

In the string of "heads" with matching "bodies," none is more inclusive than the list which St. Paul marshals in his arguments in 1 Corinthians 11:3. Look at it, strung out in separate image lines:

Now I want you to realize that
the head of every man is Christ,
and the head of the woman is man,
and the head of Christ is God.

Visualize it this way:

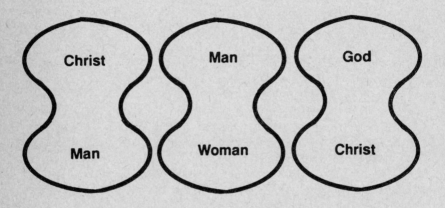

Only God and Woman are left in "single category" boxes.
Christ is sometimes head and in another relationship is body.
Man appears in both head and body positions, depending on
the relationship. If "physiology is analogical to theology,"
then we may want to examine the portable roles as we contemplate the relationships. And if the marital metaphor is
turned into theology, then "two become one," so the roles of
"head" and "body" are less important to the participants
than to spectators.

We have watched now for several months as Karen
Carpenter has stood by Ellis. His spine was crushed while
he was working on a missions project in Tennessee. Karen
has stood by her husband first in Knoxville's Fort Sanders
Presbyterian Hospital, and now more recently at Shepherd
Spinal Center in Atlanta. Who knows how long the "roles"
must be revised? But it is clear in watching them that the
tragedy is redefining "function" and "role" within a profoundly deep relationship that is flexible enough to adapt to

any demand. We know that we are watching a scene which is pregnant with metaphoric lessons for us all: The roles don't matter at all when something simply must be done.

We saw the "role shift" all played out for us before. We saw a "head" determined to empower his "body" to take his place. We saw him divest himself of temporal roles and relationships, intentionally confining himself. We saw him distribute authority and responsibility to the "body," and to do so without "divorcing" himself from the body, only confining, restricting, and removing himself temporarily. We are looking at Jesus. You can read the amazing sequence of the transfer of authority everywhere, but it is most powerfully condensed in John 13–20.

Jesus, the head, took the servant-submissive role. Read the remarkable context for the final meal Jesus asked for with the disciples. Ponder the complicated but profound sentence which traces his "descent" to servant submission:

> Jesus, fully aware that the Father had put all things under his power, and that he had come from God, and was going back to God, got up from the meal, took off his outer clothing, and wrapped a towel around his waist. Then he poured water into a basin and began to wash his disciples' feet, drying them with the towel that was wrapped around him.
>
> John 13:3–5

The summons is deafening: "If you would be a servant-submissive person, you must be 'fully aware' of three critical things about yourself." The sum of the three constitute the finest test ever devised for measuring "ego strength" or "identity."

1. *Jesus knew what his vocation was.* He knew "that the Father had put all things under his power." People who are grasping for power and are putting people under them are, no doubt without exception, insecure people who have no clear vision of what their calling, vocation, or life-task is in God's design. Such people may be heard to exclaim, "I would not be caught dead unplugging the toilet! That is janitor's work." Or, "Change a diaper? That's woman's work!" But people who know what their life-task is—their settled

calling and vocation—can do any menial task on earth. They are not confused, as insecure people are, perhaps, into believing that their work determines their worth. They are the only truly free people. You have seen them now and then, but they are rare. And they are so at ease that they may embarrass you by their readiness to perform some "inappropriate" task, something, as you would say, "beneath" them, simply because someone needs to do it.

Jesus was in a situation where someone had to do something! People of wealth hired a servant to wash everybody's feet as they stepped into the guest house. Feet were often bloodied from road wear, but were *always* dusty in a pre-concrete, pre-asphalt era. And to "lie at table" meant having your feet under someone's face and in close contact with the clothing of your "next right" partner. Spending an evening trying to eat with unwashed feet only a few inches below your place at the table could make for a most unpleasant evening. Someone had to wash the feet. Who would be more aware of the urgency of the situation than the host of the meal? The disciples had recently been upset by the rivalry over prized seats in the coming kingdom. "Status and power" were likely lingering in their minds. So Jesus did what had to be done. Peter objected, and the humorous exchange about feet versus whole body, tells us that Peter was more in touch with the significance of what was going on than the others seem to have been.

2. *Jesus knew where he came from:* "Jesus, well aware that he had come from God." Identity is deeply grounded in a sense of history, continuity, and linkage with "roots." It would be easy to miss the significance of this part of the identity package if we dismiss it as only a theological statement about Jesus' divine origin. It is that, of course, but it is so much more. What were the stories Mary and Joseph told Jesus about his conception, birth, and childhood? What stories did your parents tell you? And how do you think such a "sense of history" might affect interpersonal relationships and "management style"? Watch the ruthless executives and violent, hurtful spouses, and ask about their "roots." Are they people who missed the "blessing" of an infancy and childhood surrounded by spoken affirmation, rehearsal

of their "story," and by the magic touch of affection?[2] Was
their family system disrupted by death, divorce, or by abuse
or silence? The "high achievers" both in public and in private circles, including the religious organizations, tend to
have deep trauma, even tragedy, fueling them in their quest
for "a little more status and a little more power," often in a
hopeless quest of proving to a distant or even dead parent
that they have earned their right to worth.

3. *Jesus knew where he was going; he had a sense of destiny:* "Jesus, knowing that he was going back to God." We
can indulge in silly and dangerous competition and other
games if we lose sight of the "big picture." The big picture
requires a sense of perspective: "A hundred years from now
no one will know the difference!" But the big picture simply must also have a clear focus on the ultimate Reality, the
final goal. So we need always to be controlled by the long
view. "What kind of a marriage is this that God has given
us? How we reach the goal of the marriage is really as essential as the fact that we can see the goal. We must not
contradict our vision by the way we treat each other." Or,
"The mission of the congregation is controlling us, therefore
we cannot deal disrespectfully with one another in competitive and petty games without forfeiting our long-range vision." Violent "means" always blow up the long-range vision
of peace.

Curiously enough, all three tests are essential to discover
whether a person is morally and spiritually "safe" to be a
leader. Does the person have a clear calling and a secure
vocation? Does the person have a clear sense both of history
and of destiny, at a personal level?

In the Great Commandment, Jesus called us to:

> Love the Lord your God
>   with all your soul, mind, and strength,
>   and love your neighbor as your self.

While the command is clearly a summons to be obeyed, the
second part is also a simple statement of psychological reality:

We will love our neighbors exactly as we love ourselves.
So, people who have unfinished business dealing with voca-

tion, with history, or with destiny, are dangerous to be around if great responsibility falls on them. Have you ever been surprised when a competent person received a promotion and seemed suddenly to become a dangerous tyrant? Or have you seen an apparently amiable young person from an affluent home take on marriage and family responsibility and turn into an abusive or irresponsible maniac? Such people are revealing that they have "unfinished business" and are not ready for great responsibility. Since most of us marry during the adventure of coming to peace about "personal identity," we tend to take some competitive, even violent, behaviors into our marriages.

Jesus offers a model of maturity, and its most visible feature is servant-submission. He even turns the spotlight on the feet cleaning episode:

> "Do you understand what I have done for you? . . .
> You call me 'Teacher' and 'Lord,' and rightly so,
>   for that is what I am.
> Now that I, your Lord and Teacher, have washed your feet,
>   you also should wash one another's feet.
> I have set you an example
>   that you should do as I have done for you . . . .
> No servant is greater than his master, ...
> Now that you know these things,
>   you will be blessed if you do them."
>
> John 13:12–17

Jesus moves to intimate vulnerability, made safe by the long-range hope. He immediately announces the coming betrayal by one from the intimate circle, but seals it with: "Love one another. As I have loved you, so you must love one another" (John 13:24). All of this teaching is then wrapped in the vision of a reunion in "Father's house," and the amazing description of the future life in intimate community unfolds in John 14.

Jesus transforms servant-submission into egalitarian community. Having accepted the responsibility of being a "head" who lives by servant-submission, Jesus inducts the remaining eleven disciples into a community of peers:

"Greater love has no one than this,
    that one lay down his life for his friends.
You are my friends if you do what I command.
I no longer call you servants,
    because a servant
    does not know his master's business.
Instead, I have called you friends,
    for everything that I learned from my Father
I have made known unto you . . . .
This is my command: Love each other."

                              John 15:13–16

The teaching about the Holy Spirit continues through John 16, then a full chapter is devoted to Jesus' prayer "that they all may be one, as we are." The betrayal and crucifixion are reported in 18 and 19. But in 20 the resurrection brings a reunion.

Jesus makes a final distribution of his authority:

"As the Father has sent me,
    I am sending you."
And with that he breathed on them and said,
"Receive the Holy Spirit.
If you forgive anyone his sins,
    they are forgiven;
if you do not forgive them,
    they are not forgiven."

                              John 20:21–23

Here is the intimate "head" forming the "body" and investing his "breath," the Holy Spirit, in the life of the continuing community of faith. The metaphor of Adam into whom God breathed the original "breath" links up with images here of the divestiture of the Groom and the investiture of the Bride.

Perhaps here are two stereophonic images which will get us back on the track in our marriages. The original Adam was split, differentiating sexuality into the original Bride and Groom, and by that physiological metaphor denoting specific gifts which belong to each. Here the ultimate Adam predicts the split between Groom and Bride as Jesus will ascend, leaving the Bride to do her work in the world. And the final consummation of all things brings the Groom back to the Bride dressed in white, but surrounded by the hosts of us who are "in Christ." So, in what sense is a husband a "head" in a marriage?

Husbands as Heads

If physiology is metaphoric to marriage and to the structure of the church, then surely we can speculate at the common sense level about possible implications. But let us not forget that the Fall stands between us and the ideal. Jesus died to "put things right," but we still stand under the terrible cloud and toxic fallout of the curse and consequences of Genesis three.

Husbands are endowed with musculature, hormones, and instincts to protect, surround, and to express affection through the acquisition of food and wealth from the outer world.[3]

Husbands, even by the unique mapping capabilities of the male brain, are experts in "periscopic" tasks of looking out, sighting potential danger or havens of peace, finding the way there and making it home again.[4]

Husbands, by the androgen bath in the fetal brain, have damaged optic systems which emerge with a "gift" of "three-dimensional perception," by which they move effectively in the booby-trapped world of moving objects and approaching dangers. Many adult women, with their undamaged brains, lack depth perception sufficient to judge the distance to an approaching clothesline, without reaching to test its location. The male brain is prepared to move on to mental operations of transformational logic which depend on "formal operations" which are three-dimensional, and will move ahead in those mathematical and other logical skills which require mental "depth perception."[5]

Husbands are assertive. Even the most introverted male, if he has a healthy sense of identity, "takes over" in the external world. He negotiates, protects, and is ready to "fight battles," for wife and children. But if even an extroverted male is insecure as to identity, history, destiny, or vocation, the healthy assertive pattern diminishes or inverts into depression or irresponsibility.

Husbands are observer-referees. Their periscopic gift is also expressed in "objectivity." In their best performances, they are arbiters of justice, slicing through conflict and hurts to settle issues in the family. Indeed, their "objectivity" tends to insulate them from feelings to such an extent that they tend to try to "solve" everything within hearing distance. "But I don't want you to tell me what to do," wives and children complain, "I just want you to listen to me." Again, the damage to the corpus callosum apparently reduces the neural linkages between right and left brain hemispheres, giving males a higher specificity in focus, but insulating them from much of their own feelings in those tasks which call for "analytical" processing. On the other hand, tell a man a story, and his analysis shuts down. He is helplessly caught up with feeling. Nathan the prophet used a story to confront King David; the monarch was trapped with his defenses down. Jesus used stories to teach, and attracted large numbers of men to radical obedience and faith. Indeed, men are so starved for affective "content" that they huddle in groups to "tell stories" to each other, a phenomenon which simply does not occur at any significant level with women.

No doubt the "differentiated" list could go on and on. It is enough if we can see that anatomy and physiology establish some intrinsic differences which equip males to present gifts to their marriages and their workplaces. It is tragic, however, that these same gifts when driven by damaged ego and tragic insecurity, become tools of violence. Such exploitive behaviors are under God's judgment, of course, but they must come under our canopy of grace as targets for God's healing and transforming grace. Those of us men who suffer from ego-damage must become candidates for healing and wholeness in the community of faith.

What emerges, in such a picture of husbands, however, are the male gifts which stand behind the popular stereotypes. If we can see their behavior patterns as "expressions of gifts" instead of "cultural baggage," we may be on our way to synchronizing our marriages and our male-female relationships everywhere based on respect instead of on labeling or on competition. Men will be obligated to cut the nerve of the Marlboro man stereotype, setting them free to be "real men" in the gentlest, respect-based roles they can develop. But women will want to drop back and end the assault on masculinity that is rooted in physiology.

Healthy husbands are submissive servants, involuntarily and helplessly committed to protection, support, and care, even at the cost of laying down their health, their very life. Jesus did it for his Bride, the church!

Where There Is a Dead Head

Husbands, in most every culture, are the "family identity." Lose or change "heads" and the surviving family undergoes major, often traumatic, disruption of the family system.

We visited the hospital where Glenn lay comatose. A severe head injury in a car crash had been treated, death averted, but the vital signs predicted no recovery of consciousness. We knew Glenn as a recently graduated high school athlete. There was not a mark on that well-formed body which lay there in the intensive care unit. Only the head was injured. But across the months we watched the body soften, then begin its slow degenerative process.

Glenn's anatomical case was one in which the body simply could not replace the critical functions of the head, but the loss was not simply to the head. The body was dying, too.

So also, marriages with a dysfunctional "head" become haunted by a slow but certain death. And congregations whose "head" is some deformity of Christ the Head, are attached to a dysfunctional, likely dangerous, lethally insane head.

We commonly describe a person as "wrong headed" about lifestyle, about diet, or about some critical decision. Perhaps the metaphor signals that there are times when we need to check the "body" and "head" relationships. To become "right headed" might mean to recognize the true and healthy "head" available to us. When we say "Christ is the Head of this home," that may be the first step toward a reorganization of our marriages. And when Christ is not the head of the family, it will be likely that the husband will have a hard time fulfilling the servant-submission responsibilities that come with the territory of being regarded by wife and children as "head."

Dorothy Sayers has outlined what she calls the "humiliations of God." There are three. First, God stooped to meet us in the Incarnation, by which Jesus was stripped of the privileges of deity and entered into our human existence. In the second humiliation, the crucifixion, God became sin for us and took its consequences: death. But the greatest humiliation of God is the church. God has chosen to express himself on earth through embarrassingly imperfect humans, and he calls us his body.

The life of the body depends on attachment to the right head. In the case of Jesus, the Lord of the Church, health to the body is inevitable if we stay connected to the Head. He waits to breathe on us and infuse us with his Spirit— bringing life, harmony, and wholeness.

In much the same way, every husband finds that his most comprehensive and widest witness is in his body. Wife and children win him the widest reputation, are his truest expression. He simply depends on them more than he knows. His only hope is that there is no dysfunctional connection between body and head, leaving him morally or spiritually comatose in a world where so much needs yet to be done and which calls him to the fullest expressions of "whole person" life.

In this chapter, we have wanted you to explore the simplest possible interpretation of the basic "head" and "body" metaphor which the New Testament uses to describe both Christ–church and husband–wife relationships. We need not press the analogy to any absurdity, but we must not miss the obvious messages which arise out of the imagery given us from Creation until now.

QUESTIONS PEOPLE ASK

Q: It sounds like you do not object to males doing masculine things and females doing feminine things. Aren't you coming back "full circle" to the traditional male-female roles?

A: What we are eager to change are the unthinking stereotypes which run this way: "All women are . . ." and "All men are . . . ." But what we are eager to support is the pattern of "going with your intrinsic gifts." While these tend to follow lines of sexual differentiation, they do not do so universally. And under emergency circumstances, any woman may easily adapt to doing things for which most men are more commonly equipped, and vice versa. All of this, we hope, opens up a great deal of "cross-over" role flexibility. We celebrate the increasingly important role of "fathering" in the younger generations, and the increasing respect for women in a wide range of vocations and for their new partnership role in love and marriage.

In all of this, we simply want to keep going "back to Creation" to discover our mutual dependency, but also to go "back to Creation" to celebrate our fairly typical sex differences.

Q: *You use a term that eludes me. What is a Marlboro man?*

A: Marlborough cigarettes, when they were introduced, attracted a very small line of customers, mostly university educated types. After all, who knew how, for sure, to pronounce the name? A market research report urged two things: Change the name to one which was simple to read and to pronounce. Evoke an image of toughness and macho masculinity, since they tend to be an important part of the cigarette consumption population. So "Marlboro" became the spelling, and the unshaven, tough cowboy with the desert tough environment as the backdrop became the image. We use the term, therefore, to mean "intentional strutting in exaggerated and deformed male behaviors in order to 'prove' masculinity."

11

"Body": Another Name
for Wives?

Δ

Mark was perhaps four or five years older than I. In our
thinly populated farming community in Kansas, everybody
knew him. When any of us visited Mark's home we quickly
forgot any pity we might have brought along. This wizard of
a boy had mastered Erector construction, short-wave radio,
and electronic recording well ahead of anybody else. Educated at home before "home schooling" was any kind of fad,
Mark was mastering things other school boys never heard of.

This impressive genius was housed in a body which jerked
intermittently with involuntary spasms. Mark's head was un-
certainly balanced, bobbing at all angles irregularly, with
mouth and speech control contorted. His hands worked
jerkily, and only with enormous concentration and effort.

I thought of Mark when reading Paul Brand's review of a
television meeting of two young people in the grip of cerebral palsy. A young man was on camera who had made astonishing progress. He could spell out words using foot gestures
on the floor. He could actually activate a typewriter and
write using his toe to trigger a gadget connected to the
specific keys. The other television guest, a young woman,

155

had been placed in a mental patient hospital because no other Ohio agency had facilities for her extended care.

The young woman, like her male counterpart, made involuntary facial grimaces, drooled, and was in every way cataleptic. She had had no rehabilitation therapy except for a large wall chart divided into eighty squares with stems and completions for her ideas. When asked if she had any questions to ask the young man with his typewriter, she convulsed, eyes dancing. A volunteer from her hospital read her eyes as she communicated through her chart. Nearly five minutes later she had asked him her question: "Were . . . you . . . angry?"[1]

No doubt Mark's parents and his family heard his expressions of anger and frustration. Today, since Mark's parents are deceased, he is a patient in a rest home where his care must often match that of the Ohio girl. His disabilities of body are so pronounced as to evoke the assumption that he is something less than a person. Yet it is only his body and his body-to-nervous-system connections that are impaired. I doubt that our community has produced a brighter son.

What a Body Does Best

The body is almost everything, looking at a person objectively. Photographers commonly lop off feet to get a "close up." And because we attach a great deal of importance to the "appendage" on the other end of the body, it is rarely omitted from photographs of your favorite people. One of the most amazing color slides in our collection comes from our dozen years with wall-to-wall teenagers from the church at Winona Lake. One Hallowe'en a whole parade of teens came through doing the "trick or treat" tour. Barb Retzman and Jane Pengelly showed up in such outlandish Munchkin gear that Robbie sent me for the camera. I took them to the landing between the two levels of the house, and shot them with flash. When the slides came back here they were: no heads! I had been so obsessed with getting their Munchkin bodies in the shot that I had lopped off the heads. But the frame was literally full of that pair of Munchkin bodies. So, speaking proportionately, the body is almost everything.

The body does most of the work. An "able bodied" person is one who has no handicapping condition. Effective use of hands and feet commonly guarantees that a person can learn to perform virtually any task. Indeed, for most of human history most work has been done "by hand," and human accomplishments have been measured in "feet." "Hand made" long was the only means of production. Today it denotes either necessity or first quality, "custom made."

The body processes are also work horses. Not only are hands and feet a matter of body, the heavy duty processes of digestion, respiration, circulation, reproduction, and excretion are carried out here.[2]

The body is so treasured, so privately held, that it is shrouded, clothed to keep it from being exploited. "Naked, but unashamed" denotes the marital transparency and full trust, but in the outer world the body is clothed. This enormous "foundation" of personhood, on which nutrition, health, and continuous energizing depends, is most vitally "the self," even "the private and secret self."

Yet it is impossible to think of a body without its head attached, synchronized with every body feeling, function, and need. We indulge in this kind of "cracking the code of the head-body metaphor" only because the New Testament images have been so badly abused. The nearly absurd rehearsal of body and head functions as gifts of personhood may be useful in knocking out of our minds the Chief Executive Officer/Subservient Inferior Employee notions which have somehow migrated to the New Testament imagery.

What a Body Needs Most

Glenn in the deep coma, parts of the brain dead, or Mark with his body poorly connected to the brain are living reminders that "connectedness" and "synchronicity" with a head are essential for the body to survive, to live and move with any effectiveness.

The head is the center of the nervous system which spreads throughout the body. The head with its neurological symphony playing endlessly is not isolated off in a white bone box as the "top appendage." It is omnipresent, down to the end joint of the smallest finger or toe. The "nerves" while technically in the body are, in fact, extensions of the brain. Tom Michalko who starred in *Bonding: Relationships in the Image of God*[3] as one of two anonymous "anomalous dominance" cases, recently survived a head-on car-truck collision. A severe blow to the front of the right hemisphere put him in a deep coma. Almost our entire "spiritual formation group" huddled at the University of Kentucky emergency unit while a neurosurgeon checked his "head-body" connections. We would not see his eyes open for nearly ten days. But in those first hours before immobilizing him for the extreme measures of reconstruction, the neurosurgeon checked him out. As the doctors pinched his extremities, Tom would slap the irritated area, consistently following the doctor's check points. In spite of a major concussion, a fractured vertebra in the neck, a broken left leg, and a complete shattering of the facial bone structure, including the upper jaw, we were assured that the prognosis for significant recovery was good.

The head houses the major sense centers for collecting data essential to moment-by-moment safety and progress. This "periscope" is conveniently hoisted by the body to a position of vulnerability but of enormously fine perspective. And while the head thus signals the body to protect the whole person: "See that broken pavement! Shift right!" the body is all the while giving major signals of internal personal need: hunger, thirst, heat, or cold. Aside from hat, muffs, and coat collar, the head remains largely exposed to all weather and other hazards.

The head also is the major transmitter of personal messages. The eyes speak, but the mouth is the open megaphone to report not only what the head thinks, but what the body cries out. Except in rare cases of low self-esteem or shame, the face remains naked. Even so, "facial language" typically gives the secrets away. Last week while lecturing at a university in Michigan I read pain on Robbie's face. It was persisting for three weeks in spite of two medical visits and one prescription of antibiotics. What she was unwilling for me to know about her severe abdominal pain was showing through on her face. I was intent on getting a diagnosis, if necessary, by working backward to eliminate possibilities by a series of separate tests: appendix, ovaries, kidneys, colon. Back at the room, packing to load the car, I plied her with questions. But her pain-riddled face had already cancelled our plans to go to Niagara Falls for three days of vacation. We would return to Kentucky for additional medical consultation and tests. This much pain was too much, and it was being telegraphed from her face.

The New Testament "head-body" metaphor is so simple as to be impossible to miss. Neither "head" nor "body" is viable alone. For either to assume an adversary position to the other reduces the person to a spastic, convulsive condition. Heads that ignore bodies are in big trouble, and bodies that cut off their heads for spite have reduced themselves to another kind of existence altogether, if at all.

Watch a Body at Work

Since "head-body" is St. Paul's metaphor, primarily, it is only right to let him show us how the body works. Remember that Paul works a double metaphor in Ephesians to let the "head-body" image represent two mysteries: the relationship between Christ and the church and the relationships between a husband and a wife. St. Paul, like any of us, has no interest in making any two statements exactly the same. He uses his metaphors with some fluidity. In Ephesians 5 Christ is head and the church is body, requiring both to serve in separate roles. But in 1 Corinthians 12, Paul uses "body" as "church" and goes on to cite both features of head and body in the church. He will finally say, "Now you are the body of Christ, and each one of you is a part of it," but here in 1 Corinthians 12 that "body" includes eyes and ears.

Paul is trying to establish a coherent picture of how the Holy Spirit's gifts "fit together" for the common good of the faith community:

There are different kinds of gifts, but the same Spirit. There are different kinds of service, but the same Lord. There are different kinds of working, but the same God works all of them in all men . . . .

The body is a unit, though it is made up of many parts; and though all its parts are many, they form one body. So it is with Christ. For we were all baptized by one Spirit into one body—whether Jews or Greeks, slave or free—and we were all given the one Spirit to drink.

How more elegantly and eloquently could anyone describe the mutual dependency and the symphonic unity of the "head-body" kind of a marriage or a faith community? But even more provocatively, Paul goes on to describe conflict, paralysis, and spastic body life, especially that rooted in feelings of inferiority or in domineering "parts" which "put down" the others:

Now the body is not made up of one part but of many. If the foot should say, "Because I am not a hand, I do not belong to the body," it would not for that reason cease to be part of the body. And if the ear should say, "Because I am not an eye, I do not belong to the body," it would not for that reason cease to be part of the body. If the whole body were an eye, where would the sense of hearing be? If the whole body were an ear, where would the sense of smell be? But in fact God has arranged the parts in the body, every one of them, just as he wanted them to be. If they were all one part, where would the body be? As it is, there are many parts, but one body.

And what does our treatment of our bodies tell us about where the real honor and deference goes? Who gets the lion's share of the clothing budget? Head or body? And why?

The eye cannot say to the hand, "I don't need you!" And the head cannot say to the feet, "I don't need you!" On the contrary, those parts of the body that seem to be weaker are indispensable, and the parts that we think are less honorable we treat with special honor. And the parts that are unpresentable are treated with special modesty, while our presentable parts need no special treatment. But God has combined the members of the body and has given greater honor to the parts that lacked it, so that there should be no division in the body, but that its parts should have equal concern for each other. If one part suffers, every part suffers with it; if one part is honored, every part rejoices with it.

There it is again. Everywhere it is the same: co-regency, joint-tenancy, joint-heirs: "Its parts . . . have equal concern for each other." Suffering or celebration affect the whole person, not just the part being attacked or honored.

> Now you are the body of Christ, and each one of you is a part of it. And in the church God has appointed first of all apostles, second prophets, third teachers, then workers of miracles, also those having gifts of healing, those able to help others, those with gifts of administration, and those speaking in different kinds of tongues. Are all apostles? Are all prophets? Are all teachers? Do all work miracles? Do all have gifts of healing? Do all speak in tongues? Do all interpret? But eagerly desire the greater gifts. And now I will show you the most excellent way.

And Paul goes on to define "the way of love," or "charity" as the King James Version called it. This absolute "equal concern for each other" that he speaks of in 12:25 is amplified by the entirety of 1 Corinthians 13—the "most excellent way"!

"You are the body of Christ." Paul is adamant, redundant, in one metaphoric exclamation or another. But here the absolute common value to the various gifts within the body add up to the enormous potential of a healthy body connected to Christ its head. And we have no trouble turning the Ephesians 5 metaphor back onto 1 Corinthians 12 to see that the husband-wife relationship is nourished and corrected by these images, as well.

Wives as Bodies

Here again physiology is analogical to a theological mystery. How wives are understood, valued, and appreciated by the image of "body."

Wives are, in fact, "bodies." Even at its grossest distortion, male attention to women is to refer to a woman as "a body!" "What a body!" may be exploitive blasphemy, but if so, it turns out also to be the "lowest form of theology." Exactly. Elegant, magnetically attractive to the male, women appeal to men for deeper reasons than they know. From Eden until now, men "leave father and mother" and follow the magnet until they "cleave to" their woman whom they know to be at one with their bodies, either in holy mystery or in earthly blasphemy. It is a matter of moving from one dependency to another. What good is all of that male assertiveness, energy, and vitality without a "body"?

Women are endowed with broader, more integrated perceptual abilities than are men. Perhaps because of the undamaged, highly lateralized brain,[4] their reasoning is intuitive and global instead of the more masculine pattern of linear analytical reasoning. The intuitive operation streaks at a high speed and requires major access to the right hemisphere. Left-handed men tend to make intuitive judgments which resemble women's reasoning, as do artists and musicians whose vocations keep them "in their right minds" for major swatches of time. But all of us would use intuitive judgment if we could access the brain resources to do it, because it is both faster and more accurate, in general, than mere analytical logic. One wrong piece of calculation in a complicated analytical procedure can turn up a completely wrong decision. But with intuitive, nonverbal, global collecting, the data includes past experiences, impressions, attitudinal readings, and perhaps a million perceptions which do not translate into language or numbers. And the intuitive judgment collects all of these data and spins off an almost instant reading which is astonishingly reliable.[5]

Wives are "support systems" for their husbands. At its worst, it is blind reverence and awe. In this fallen form, women blindly comply with the most corrupt, violent, and destructive of schemes their husbands suggest. When the Genesis 3 warning, "her desire shall be to her husband," is reigning, a woman may forfeit responsibility, "roll over and play dead," and in every way "cop out" on "having dominion," even over her own life. Yet no husband can make it without the support of a good woman. And women are endowed with unusually consistent patterns of serving, equipping, and nurturing. These "maternal" gifts more often are delivered in the support of a beloved husband than in the service of offspring. Here again, an intrinsic gift likely stands behind the often abusive cultural stereotype which expects or demands that a woman do all the serving: the food catering, the coffee making, the secretarial recording, everything! It is criminal if we enforce the stereotype, but it is absurd to deny the grandeur of a creation which endows us with gifts to offer each other.

Wives are for people! Taken as a group, women make decisions more often than men on the basis of "how it will affect the people involved." While they are "objective-referee" types, women tend to be "subjective concerned" people. It is a gift, and the perspective of "people concerns" is badly needed in any decision-making environment. But a certain vulnerability comes with the "people concern" territory, too. It shows up as an inappropriate level of concern for "what people think," but also as a sometimes neurotic pity for people in trouble. The strength of the "people concern" gift shows as a wife looks after the human cargo in the entire family, including the husband. She is more likely than he to be sensitive to his health and physical welfare. She knows when he needs a holiday or a honeymoon. And her gift of feeling what others feel extends to the widest circle of contacts. No wonder Jesus called the church his "body," given the mission of the Christian faith—to wrap arms around the poor, the dying, the sinners, and the innocent.

What emerges in the image of wives as bodies is the clear picture of the selfless gift of strength, support, and concern which they bring to every situation, within the family and beyond. Healthy wives are submissive supporters who gladly fuse their identity with that of husband and of family. They are virtually helplessly committed to the supportive care of people close to them. They give themselves to their husbands, just as the church is called to give itself entirely to Jesus.

In this chapter we have wanted you to look at the "body" part of the "head-body" image in the New Testament. But we wanted you to also keep a focus on "body as wife." We are concerned, also, to shut down false images of "submission" which suggest inferiority or passivity. It is exhilarating to see St. Paul's more complete description of how the body works—as a unity, with absolute mutual respect and mutual experience. So this is our gift to you here.

QUESTIONS PEOPLE ASK

Q: How would you suggest that I cope with a husband who believes he is following the Bible when he is a lone ranger, authoritarian "head of the house"?

A: Do everything you can to support his hunger and thirst for God and for knowledge of the Bible. Christian submission is a lovely principle that will allow you to affirm him in his growing sensitivity, and to ignore or accept the consequences of his more blind brutality points. And submission is not passive or fatalistic. It always hopes for transformation and growth. So get your own sensitivity down the line in its development. Pose questions and problems now and then for this Master-head of yours. And while he comes to his own awakening, find ways to be a healthy "body," to nourish and support everything you can to lift the pressure and a potentially impossible burden from your husband. Omniscience and omnipotence are a very heavy load to carry.

12

The New Adam: From Image to Likeness?

△

When Eugene O'Neill put theological lines in the mouth of his main character in Act Four, Scene One of *The Great God Brown*, he stumbled intuitively on what many of us have hoped and others of us have been studying empirically. He said:

> This is Daddy's bedtime secret for today:
> "Man is born broken.
> He lives by mending.
> The grace of God is glue!"

Life is a pilgrimage of one kind or another. There is no question but that we are all imprinted with God's image as an enormous potentiality. But we are also flawed. We have deformed ideas about ourselves and about other people. We are "egocentric" and imagine ourselves as the center of the universe. This "self-centered" vision puts us into deformed relationships. A marriage which brings together two "egocentric" people will have conflict, competition, and a "win or lose" complex hanging over much of the relationship. Still the participants are God's "imaged" participants: they have

165

a sense of justice, an awareness of good and evil, the power
of moral choice, and they represent God within the earthly
Creation. But they may, with that moral endowment, de-
scend into increasingly violent, abusive, and destructive patterns of choice and life. On the other hand, they may
become increasingly reflective, increasingly aware of their
own tendency to be self-centered, and increasingly penitent
before the God whose image they bear. These folks will be
open to grace and the transformation which Jesus, the Second Adam, can bring. In a word, they are being transformed
into the likeness of God, and the basic image is the raw material with which grace is at work sanctifying them and moving them in the trajectory toward wholeness.

A Story of Reflection and Transformation

Working as we do within a "developmentalist" and a
"transformationalist" perspective, we are always seeing patterns of pilgrimage in people's life stories. Today at breakfast
Brian told us the story of his transformation. As a college
freshman at a Colorado public university, he "dropped into
the hole of life," he said. We asked whether he was spelling
that "whole" or "hole." He smiled and rushed ahead with his
story. Transferring to Greenville College, his Dad's alma
mater, he became angry and disorderly. But in desperation
he gathered three other hellions together and they started a
Bible study where they expressed their cynicism. Within a
semester the group had expanded to more than two dozen.
We thought of John Westerhoff's thesis that we need to
"baptize doubt" and give our young people a "blessing" to
pursue truth vigorously and with a hermeneutic of suspicion.
So Brian came to faith that way. He is being married next
week and will return after the honeymoon to continue his
study for the pastoral ministry with us.

In another century John Wesley was a classical example of
the O'Neill pattern of "being born broken, spending life
mending, with God's grace as the glue." Since John Wesley
kept a journal, he was programming himself for reflection,
which is an essential prerequisite to transformation. Here
are lines lifted from the published version of this Anglican

priest's *Journal*. The entries are all written with the reflection time of most of a long life behind him:

> I believe, till I was about ten years old, I had not sinned away that "washing of the Holy Ghost" which was given me in baptism; having been strictly educated and carefully taught that I could only be saved "by universal obedience, by keeping all the commandments of God"; in the meaning of which I was diligently instructed. And those instructions, so far as they respected outward duties and sins, I gladly received and often thought of. But all that was said to me of inward obedience or holiness I neither understood nor remembered. So that I was indeed as ignorant of the true meaning of the law as I was of the gospel of Christ.
>
> The next six or seven years [ages 11–17] were spent at school; where outward restraints being removed, I was much more negligent than before, even outward duties, and almost continually guilty of outward sins, which I knew to be such, though they were not scandalous in the eye of the world. However, I still read the Scriptures, and said my prayers morning and evening. And what I now hoped to be saved by, was, (1) not being so bad as other people; (2) having still a kindness for religion; and (3) reading the Bible, going to church, and saying my prayers.
>
> Being removed to the University for five years [to about age 22], I still said my prayers both in public and in private, and read, with the Scriptures, several other books of religion, especially comments on the New Testament. Yet I had not all this while so much as a notion of inward holiness; nay, went on habitually, and for the most part very contentedly, in some or other known sin: indeed, with some intermission and short struggles, especially before and after the Holy Communion, which I was obliged to receive thrice a year. I cannot well tell what I hoped to be saved by now, when I was continually sinning against that little light I had; unless by those transient fits of what many divines taught me to call repentance.
>
> When I was about twenty-two, my father pressed me to enter into holy orders [licensing toward ordination]. At the same time, the providence of God directed me to Kempis's Christian Pattern. I began to see that true religion was seated in the heart and that God's law extended to all our thoughts, as well as words and actions. I was, however, very angry at Kempis for being too strict; though I read him only in Dean Stanhope's

translation. Yet I had frequently much sensible comfort in reading him, such as I was an utter stranger to before; and meeting likewise with a religious friend, which I had never had till now, I began to alter the whole form of my convocation, and to set in earnest upon a new life. I set apart an hour or two a day for religious retirement. I communicated [took Holy Communion] every week. I watched against all sin, whether in word or deed. I began to aim at, and pray for, inward holiness. So that now, "doing so much, living so good a life," I doubted not but I was a good Christian.[1]

John Wesley describes the rigid, legalistic, passively violent clergyman that he was as he approached the age of thirty:

In my youth I was not only a member of the Church of England [Anglican], but a bigot of it, believing none but the members of it to be in a state of salvation . . . . I began to abate of this violence in 1729 . . . . But still I was as zealous as ever, observing every point of Church discipline, and teaching all my pupils so to do . . . . When I was abroad [as a missionary to America], I observed every rule of the Church, even at the peril of my life . . . . I was exactly of the sentiment when I returned from America.[2]

Finally, on the evening of May 24, 1738, at the age of thirty-four years, eleven months, John Wesley reports:

I went very unwillingly to a society in Aldersgate Street, where one was reading Luther's preface to the *Epistle to the Romans*. About a quarter before nine, while he was describing the change which God works in the heart through faith in Christ, I felt my heart strangely warmed. I felt that I did trust in Christ, Christ alone for salvation; and an assurance was given me that he had taken away *my* sins, even *mine*, and saved *me* from the law of sin and death . . . . And herein I found the difference between this and my former state chiefly consisted. I was striving, yea, fighting with all my might under the law, as well as under grace. But then I was sometimes, if not often, conquered; now, I was always conqueror.[3]

This was not the end of the "pilgrimage" for John Wesley. His journal and private diary are dotted with further transformations, and a letter to his brother on December 15, 1772, notes a low point from which he longs for the security of the legalism of his old University years: "I often cry out, 'My former happy life restore!' Let me be again an Oxford Methodist! I am often in doubt whether it would not be best for me to resume all my Oxford rules, great and small."

What had John Wesley been doing instead of passively continuing in the security of his legalistic years? He had been the instrument of revival and awakening on two continents. And his simple "rule" for obedience to God was to live out what he called "perfect love." It consisted of following two principles in which Jesus boiled down all the law and the prophets: "Love God with all your heart, soul, mind, and strength, and love your neighbor as you love yourself."

And on another occasion in 1766, John Wesley confided in another letter to Charles revealing how complicated his pilgrimage was. This time he was likely classically depressed. Yet his integrity, God's holiness magnetically working in him, "held him to the course."

Pilgrimage, People, and Holiness

We have summarized the John Wesley story of a spiritual pilgrimage to suggest that many of us have (1) egocentric, (2) legalistic, and (3) principled epochs in our life history. It is not difficult to imagine that our marriages are going to be formed within the boundaries of our personal orientation, at a given moment within our two pilgrimages. What this might mean is that if two partners are at the same point in the three-level journey, we can anticipate what the structure and expectations of their marriage may be at that point. Let's try an outline of the main patterns that might emerge:

Egocentric Period: Each has a personal, selfish agenda. Relationship at best is a "mutually beneficial" package: I'll scratch your back; you scratch mine. At worst, it is a competitive and adversarial game, with a wide range of battle wounds which may scar the marriage in the long term.

Legalistic Period: Roles are rigidly defined. Labor is divided. Expectations are enforced. Rewards accompany compliance with role and task assignment. Blame is fixed and penalties assessed for failure to fulfill and keep within the role assignment. Emphasis is on further clarifying roles and work assignments. Typically the man becomes the expert on "rights of men," and the woman studies the "rights and roles of women."

Principled Period: Emphasis is on the totality of the marriage, the combined assets when all of the gifts are being discovered and put to the best use. Each acts to protect and enhance the other. Roles are fluid; tasks which need to be done deserve help and cooperation from the spouse as often as possible. Intimacy is the primary agenda, since conflict no longer consumes the energy once used in maintaining roles and task distinctions and blowing the whistle on failure. Communication keeps unfinished business and passive aggression from consuming time and energy.

In a word, married people spend most of their time focused on issues appropriate to the level of their pilgrimage:

1. Egocentric agenda: Having fun, being fulfilled.
2. Legalistic agenda: Defining roles, asserting rights.
3. Principled agenda: Growing together, celebrating life.

Again, the "stages" of a marriage might be categorized in this way:

1. Egocentric Stage: Symbiotic/Adversary Relationship
2. Legalistic Stage: Conventional Roles—Rights Positioning
3. Principled State: Whole Persons/Each *for* the Other

We speculate that marriage is probably the primary curriculum God gives most people for accelerating the spiritual journey. (We shudder to think that we might have become "arrested" and stuck in either of the early stages of our marriage.) So in this chapter we want to report where we are now, on the eve of our fortieth anniversary—which will arrive technically on July 15, 1988! And we will try to reflect and to describe some of the triggers which released us from our tendency to get "stuck" in a stagnant and habituated marriage.

An egocentric, symbiotic/adversary stage in a marriage tends to be built around stereotypes and expectations which "serve the self," typically justifying those expectations by appealing to tradition or to fragments of authoritative statements selectively used to cement the egocentric argument. This naïve, primitive, and fallen sort of marital symbiosis shows up almost inevitably when we poll junior high teens. Recently a dozen teens responded to our questions: "What do you like most about being a man? . . . about being a woman?" In more than half of the responses there was a clear statement from the young men, "Being the boss, being in charge, having a lot of freedom to do what I want to do." That is clearly rooted in the original sin if it involves manip- ulation, use, or "ownership" of another person. The young women stopped us cold, "So I don't really have to make de- cisions, have a lot of responsibility; so I'll have somebody to take care of me." You don't have to be Joseph in Egypt to read those dreams and to guarantee that they can easily come true. John MacArthur is exactly right when he points out that no matter how "co-equal" a marriage may begin, it will turn quickly into a vertical power-play. A famous comic strip shows two stone age women conspiring: "I'll tell you what we'll do. We'll roll over and play dead and let them think they are the boss. Then we'll nag the suckers into sub- mission!" Exactly: "Adversary-ship."

A legalistic/silent truce stage in a marriage is a cold stand- off. While the egocentric couple may continue to play ro- mantic and flirtatious games, each looking out for personal desires, the legalistic couple has cooled off. They have re- sorted to proof-texting their roles and rights in a marriage. As they appeal to authority, often fragments of the Bible, they are reduced to rather stiff marionette-behaving people who are "going through the motions" of a marriage, but spontaneous and deep intimacy are evaporating from the former egocentric, playful stage.

Typically there are children by now, and day after day consists primarily of "maintenance" duties and responsibili- ties. There has been an unspoken truce to the effect that we know what our roles and relationships are; and we are too busy keeping the family afloat to try to improve or enrich the marriage right now. So "don't rock the boat."

There is a large dose of self-pity in this legalistic stage. Each may take pride in "being a good husband" or "a good wife," but affection is scarce, and the pain of a marginally dysfunctional sexual relationship is close to the surface. Typically, "mid-life" is just around the corner. Such a marriage is ripe for an alien bond to steal away one or both of the partners from their once intense attraction, satisfaction, and pleasure with each other.

In *Lovers—Whatever Happened to Eden?* we have wanted to share the story of our marriage. It has been far from perfect, yet the stages have surely been there. We think of it as "the pilgrimage of a growing marriage." So in this last chapter we want to tell you where we are today, to look back at the last major transition point. We feel less certain how to describe the marriage we have today than those two previous stages. You may see things in what we report here that we do not yet see. And we cannot know whether there is yet another stage awaiting us. But we know the turf of the egocentric and the legalistic years in our relationship. We have reported those in earlier chapters. So in this final chapter let us try to describe where we are today and something of how we got there.

Robbie: From "Body" to Person

I think the first day I knew something was going to be different was the day Don asked me, somewhat desperately, whether I would take care of the monthly bills while he dug into the last half of his Ph.D. work. He was facing weekly commuting plus maintenance of a full-time denominational executive office. I was flattered, and frankly was a little eager to "try my hand" at the business side of the household. From the time we were married, Don had insisted that I have a signature on the bank account and would issue me a check whenever I needed to make a purchase. He was not stingy, though both of us have a frugal streak which we think of as "stewardship" of resources. But things did begin to change. I was good at the books, records, and accounts.

When the Kentucky call came and Don said he wanted to take the job at Asbury Seminary, I knew we were in for some major transitions. We decided that Mike and I should hold steady at Winona Lake. I could establish minimum "retirement benefits" in two years, and Mike could almost finish high school by then. So Don would commute. That would make me a "widow" for three or four days a week in the best scenario. If we put the Indiana house on the market and bought a house in Kentucky, we could see even more turbulence coming into our relatively tranquil, predictable life.

And the plot did thicken. We bought the Kentucky house. Don needed his "free days" to supervise contractors and to do some of the interior demolition and reconstruction himself. This meant Mike and I were the "commuters," going to Kentucky on Friday and returning on Sunday evenings to Winona Lake, Indiana.

If we needed a "curriculum" for transformation which included frustration, pain, and despair, we got it. Within that first full year of Don's serving full time on the faculty, I found myself presiding over: (1) The family car overheated with frozen pistons, half-way between Wilmore and Winona Lake. (2) Mike's "school car" developed radiator problems and lost anti-freeze, on a repeating basis. (3) The rural Winona Lake septic system backed up, plugged and full—a "first" for the system. (4) On one trip back north, at a fuel stop I left my purse in the women's room, returning from a half mile up the highway to find it stolen, complete with all money and credit cards as we moved north into the jaws of a blizzard and the likelihood of needing a motel for overnight. And (5) I picked up a virus near Christmas which, with the heavy antibiotics, seriously depleted my system. I looked like a ghost when Don's entire family arrived to spend Christmas with us for the last time we would be in the home we built in Indiana.

During that year I had no choice but to become a decision-maker. I had always depended on Don to take care of everything. I knew he could and would "take over" whenever anything needed to be done or decided. In some strange way, perhaps through spiritual atrophy on my part, I had been leaving the praying, seeking, and waiting before God to Don. He was indeed my "priest" in everything. I had no idea who served as his priest or mentor. It never occurred to me that God might lead me, or that I might be able to seek and to know God's will in things large and small.

I had never bought clothes, even for myself, without Don's approval. Now I found I could do that. I began taking over discipline and guidance with Mike. Before, I felt that this was Don's job and he should do it, so I had no idea I could contribute to it at all.

Having to make decisions and deal with the consequences of my own reasoning and choices changed everything. Suddenly I was aware that I wasn't so nervous about offering a contrasting perspective or opinion in a faculty meeting at school or on a church committee. I also found that I could carry on a scrappy dialogue with Don. I think he was surprised, because I knew I was invading his "turf" of decision-making. Now I was also thinking for myself. I was less intimidated by fears of offending someone and more committed to working honestly for the best outcomes by straightforward and clear-headed honesty. I found I had a good mind, that I could carry on a dialogue in the outer world.

I was beginning to develop a critical analytical ability, and that felt good. I found I could trust my intuitive judgment and could evaluate authority structures. For years, I had been a passive, silent partner, virtually a "non-participating stockholder" everywhere.

I had a greatly improved sense of my own self. I was able to release my husband and sons and not feel that I had to load my own low self-esteem on them and bind us all up with my feelings of inferiority and shame. I felt "ten feet tall," capable, competent, and a whole person before God.

After taking the Myers-Briggs personality test about eight years ago, I was enormously affirmed to find that my gifts were vastly different from Don's. I knew I had been making positive contributions to the marriage, and I was exhilarated to discover that I could be set free to make even more contributions. I knew, too, that I was not having to "re-make" Don in my image, nor would he need to remake me into his own personality profile. "Together," he once said, "we have a whole set of dominoes, but either of us alone would be operating with only half a set." This open window on the variety of God's gifts in creating personalities so different from each other, put me at ease around everyone. I could see how much I needed people who had seemed odd to me because they were different.

Don always took the initiative about church attendance. We never missed a service except for illness or our justifiable double schedule. That meant an average of five services a week, if you count Sunday school and youth meetings in which some of us were involved during our entire two decades of child-rearing and launching.

Don was reasonable, and the boys' agendas sometimes blocked out an occasional church attendance for all of us. But I never had to even so much as ask the question of whether we would be attending church. After all, Don was an ordained minister, whether serving as a pastor or as a denominational executive. It was his business to "support the system," so I accepted all of that without thinking, without discussion. And the boys did as well. None of us realized that perhaps we were "going through motions" which were not putting all of us in touch with what the real issues are. These undergird religious practices such as church attendance.

At first when Don was gone on Wednesday night, I had to decide whether to go to mid-week prayer meeting. So I quit going for a while as things got more and more complicated. Don always got us around and off to church. But when the minor catastrophes began to stack up, I turned to God for myself, to the Bible on a very systematic basis, and got a new vision of who God is. This brought church and worship and prayer meeting all into an important personal focus for me.

I also established my daily "quiet time" as a rigorous priority—out of desperation for taking responsibility for my new increased domain. Today that time has expanded substantially and includes an early morning prayer partner once each week, with a special intercessory dimension to our conversation and petition.

I sensed that our marriage was changing. I no longer watched Don so closely or worried that he might offend someone in his work as a national executive in the church. It changed my side of our relationship. I now felt like a true partner and peer. It is striking, and not at all predictable at first glance, but I found myself willing to "set him free" to be his own person. I think my sense of respect for him established a new level of trust and freedom for both of us. While I was never a smothering or jealous wife, I did "mother" Don a lot and worry about him hurting his "image" by doing something stupid. I saw that I wasn't responsible for Don's actions, nor nervous that he would offend someone. I suddenly "let him go," knowing that if he "made waves," he could also take care of them. I was "growing up." We both became "adults" in some amazing and deeply satisfying way.

The last fifteen years, however, have provided the unique crucible for growth and transformation. In a single week which typifies the ingredients of pain and challenge that stretch across the decade and a half, my father died quite suddenly, a second trauma broke in the family, and a seminary graduate couple returned to hide away in the aftershock of pastoral adultery which threatened to destroy their marriage. I found myself suddenly carrying more grief than I could handle. I turned to God and to Scripture in a new and different way. For several months, Don carried his own pain and much of mine as I withdrew in an effort to find better resources for dealing with the grief that seemed to be swallowing me.

Today, I find that I am a woman at peace with myself. I enjoy my second grade teaching, which I do for the fun of it and for the sense of wholeness I get from cranking out every morning at seven to face a room full of children. Don and I have each other, but neither of us is "dependent" for survival on the other. We celebrate the long and good years we have had, and we long for them to go on forever. But we are at peace with life and whatever comes to us.

Don: From "Head" to Person

As I try to re-trace the pattern in our marriage, I confess that on our wedding day when I was nineteen years old, I thought largely in egocentric terms. My view of my marriage was one of "taking a wife," in some literal, "gift wrapped" sense. She was a "show-piece," and many of the accessories of the marriage tradition seem to emphasize the

"bride" as "property." All of this was made secure by a legal
document which, while it conveyed no wealth to me and a
rather heavy sense of maintenance responsibility and liabil-
ity, at least "conveyed" this woman to me and actually re-
named her in a way that let me think of her as "mine" in a
tangible, chattel sense.

I am not wanting to suggest that I began to abuse her, to
treat her as a slave. But I did have heavy expectations of her
in terms of services rendered, areas of labor that were to be
executed, and long-term, the obligation to "bear my children." In our better times, I was a benevolent monarch. I
was kind to her. And I was a wise lover who tempered my
desires to fall within the limits of her interests. Yet I made
commitments on which she had to perform. I brought guests
home unannounced, for meals or overnight. I was baffled
when she would take some occasion in the presence of witnesses, especially of my family, to report anecdotes which
put me in "a bad light." It was clear that my private exploitation of her was being returned in these open efforts to hurt
me. My dictatorship was evoking some resentment. The resentment must have been squelched inside her, but when it
showed its head, I knew she had ways of "making me squirm
into compliance" with her basic desires.

A little before the age of thirty-five, I gave up on having it
my way. I still had the "ideal" marriage guiding my aspiration, but I could see that while some marriages might be
well synchronized and "everybody got what they wanted," I
was never going to have what I wanted in our marriage.
What was to be the "last whimper" of the egocentric era
came as I occasionally ventilated my frustration to Robbie.
In these episodes I exposed some streaks of self-pity by
throwing in the towel on a small handful of petty wishes
which, I could sense, were falling on deaf ears. I sensed that
things were never going to change. So I retaliated in
"reciprocity." The legalistic/silent truce era consisted of a
freeze-out: If I can't have what I want, sister, you won't get
what you want all the time, either.

I kept up my end of the family responsibility, but no
more. The distribution of labor was now set in concrete. Our
roles were well established, almost fenced apart. Now and

then we "pot-shotted" each other when some lapse of performance or some overbooked schedule messed up completion of part of the family or household responsibility. We maintained this "order" through habit mostly, but monitored it with nagging, even shouting, exchanges which evoked enough guilt to whip each other back into line.

Robbie and I had mostly good days. We had a good "functioning" marriage, but I knew this was not a mellowing and ripening marriage. We were also consumed in parenting tasks. We were fanatical about supporting our sons in their school, music, church, and athletic events—of which there were many. We were also consumed by the volunteer youth ministry responsibilities of a rather large church, and I directed between three and six choral groups every week in the church, including the Sunday morning choir with its platform responsibility. Besides these occupations, our professional vocations were advancing, claiming increasing blocks of time beyond the work day.

It was this vocational expansion that eventually was to "stress" us into the third major epoch, where we continue today. I became immersed in doctoral study at Indiana University. Robbie simultaneously began graduate work on a reading specialist's certificate. My doctoral program required a technical year of residency, but I did that by commuting from two hundred miles away. One day, I threw the checkbook on the kitchen table and said, "Would you mind paying the monthly bills until I get through this program?" I had no idea that my "surrender" of the financial management portfolio in my "sex role" assignment would be the tiny hole in the dike which would release a floodtide of changes in our marriage. Until that pivotal day, I had single-handedly managed our financial affairs, limited though they were. I literally carried the checkbook with some sense of masculine responsibility. It never occurred to me to ask Robbie to do anything financial. I was stereotyped into an absolute conformity to some "role" and responsibility pattern I had observed somewhere.

Robbie had an accounting and bookkeeping major in her undergraduate years, but I had never shared any of the family's financial management, decisions, or responsibilities with her. I bought cars, obligated income, purchased furniture, and ordered equipment without so much as reporting to her what I was doing.

When I cried for help, I still remember that she took the checkbook and said a quiet, "OK." Immediately our financial house came into order. Our checkbook and the monthly ledger sheets from the bank suddenly came into "balance" for the first time in our lives. I have never carried the checkbook since. That was in about 1968, and I was looking at age forty.

Then, in February of 1971, I began two and a half years of commuting from Winona Lake, Indiana, to Wilmore, Kentucky, each week. A death on the faculty at Asbury Theological Seminary prompted the emergency "visiting professor" call. When it turned into a full-time faculty appointment in the Fall of 1971, our household was wrenched with the decision: Should we pick up and move to Kentucky now? Several factors suggested "No" as the better answer. We had bought property in Kentucky which was in need of complete restoration. Mike was literally "crazy glued" to Warsaw Community Schools and their music and athletic programs, not to mention his friends. Robbie was within two years of meeting "minimum retirement" status for Indiana school systems. We calculated a scheme by which I could leave home on Monday morning and return on Friday night. Mike, at fifteen, was flattered at the suggestion that he would have "to look after Mother" for me. And Robbie seemed quite ready to expand her responsibilities in my absence. One semester of my emergency commuting had gone fairly smoothly.

So we found ourselves in a two-and-one-half-year "stress" period in the structure of our relationship. There were the predictable complications: car trouble, plugged-up septic system, teen agenda requests, and supervision decisions. Robbie got more than she could have anticipated in "experience" in managing the outer world for the household.

But there were astonishing and completely unpredictable benefits. I found my fondness for Robbie was energized by the four days away. I slept in a single bed in my temporary guest quarters on campus, then later in our "under renovation" home. Some nights I never even turned over and could crawl out leaving the bed looking almost newly made up. In our habituated nocturnal intimacy at home we had rolled, embraced, turned, and re-embraced a dozen times or more each night, in what must have been very light fits of sleep. Now, we had new experiences to report to each other. We were starved simply to see each other. Our affection seemed fresh and alive. We were more sexually charged than we had been in fifteen years. Suddenly we had a new marriage.

I took enormous pleasure in the excellent decisions Robbie was making when "the cookies crumbled" suddenly, demanding choice and action. "I am married to an excellent manager," I remember thinking. I hope I said it to her at the time. She is so effective in supervision that whenever we need a contractor on the job today we look at the options now open to us, and most often she gets the nod as the supervisor. Both of us can get executive work done, though we use quite different strategies in accomplishing it.

And it was clear to me that this passive, reticent woman God had so wisely brought into my life was suddenly showing signs of being a spiritual giant. In addition, I was pleased that she was being pulled onto important public school and church agencies. Within a few years of her move to Kentucky she was elected to a county position in her profession which had her repeatedly representing school concerns at the Commonwealth legislature in the state capitol. I was pleased to be her consort at official banquets where she took the lecturn, made the speeches, and handled public protocol for her domain.

Today, we have a marriage that is characterized by a solid rock base of absolute mutual respect and commitment to the other's well-being. If I am ill, Robbie sees it before I am quite aware the fever is rising. When she comes down with a virus, I get absolutely aggressive and see to it that we get medical attention. There are a thousand tasks which were once "sex-typed" into categories which we now share, or which we tip to each other depending on the immediate circumstances and available energy and time. It is clear to me that Robbie will "make a good and healthy widow" should such a lot ever come to her. She is a complete woman.

I can read Proverbs 31 today and see her face. I could even add a few lines to underscore Robbie's competence. For example, when our accountant phones our house these days, he asks to speak to Robbie. She always keys in quickly on issues he raises. And I am glad.

A Three-Stage Marriage Trajectory?

We cannot say whether every marriage will necessarily have to go through egocentric and legalistic stages. We are simply reporting that we can see those stages and can identify clear transitions between them. A more amazing discovery has dawned on us. We think that only the "principled, mutually affirming, co-regency" marriage provides a platform from which to see that there are alternate models or stages. You can't draw a map until you have been over the road! For example:

Stage One: Egocentric marriages are likely so involved in the "game of loving" that there is little concern to figure out what has happened to other folks. Most young lovers watch their parents and wonder whatever happened to love and affection. Many of them cannot imagine their parents enjoying anything resembling "making out" or "having sex." Beyond that, the young tend to have given up on making sense out of the older generation anyway, and they tend to attribute other marital patterns to the "olden days" category. The egocentric lovers are so absorbed with "getting the gusto," that so long as they can work out a reciprocal, mutually paying off relationship, they are simply indifferent to how anyone else lives. Indeed, some of them refuse to marry on the basis that they see their friends who marry moving toward painfully legalistic, role-defining and abusing marriages.

Stage Two: People who write the manuals, rules, and lists of "principles" for chain-of-command marriages have no tolerance whatever for Stage One partners or for Stage Three lovers. They are all structure, rules, and roles. And they offer only "standard models." Typically, no marriage is regarded as kosher unless it is hierarchical, with well-defined patterns of unilateral submission. The legalistic approach to any problem is to (1) study it, then (2) find the "authority" statements which seem to match your objectives, and (3) codify it, citing chapter and verse and listing the rules in numbered order. The major production of "marriage manuals" and "biblical models for the family" comes from people with this rules, regulations, authority, conflict, and command preoccupation.

One popular writer and lecturer has a new book out on the family: *Building Biblical Families*. There is a section on "God's Model Home." It is all built around his thesis which is this: "roles determine relationships." Amazing. We suspect that just the opposite is true: *relationships determine roles*. There is a major section entitled, "The Husband as Head." Although "head" is lifted from the Ephesians material, it has escaped the author that "body" is the missing ninety percent of the whole person under discussion. He develops two major sections about "head," and none about "body." It is not surprising that the author's perception of "head" is exclusively that of chief executive officer of the marriage and the family. We find it interesting that most often it is men who write or speak convincingly about "male headship" and go silent on the substantial biblical and theological contribution of the female, the feminine, and the maternal to Christian thought. Another section is entitled "The Husband as Lover." There are no sections to suggest whether the wife has any constructive role or responsibility in the "biblical family."

Stage Three. Principled lovers tend both to have set each other free and to have laid down their lives and energies to exalt the other. What is more, only they are able to look at the young, playful, egocentric crowd and celebrate their innocent games, knowing that God can lead them to richer, less manipulative agendas up the road. But the principled lovers are also able to match up their own "power and conflict" history with the popular models which stress roles and rules. These mellow couples know that some of those people, if they live long enough and suffer a little, will also break free to love without fear and without preoccupation for announcing their own status and security needs by claiming positions of superiority or inferiority.

In this chapter we have opened the most recent transformation of our marriage in a way that we have not before talked of outside our own home. Indeed, our sons and their wives have found the details of our romance and marriage most entertaining as they perused the manuscript for this book. But we have been grateful that across the years we have had three wonderful marriages, each of them different, and all have been to each other. All of them have been characterized by fidelity, affection, and unquestioned commitment to "see each other through" our lifetimes. No doubt at any moment along the pilgrimage of our marriage we would have claimed that "the present is the best." And we can, based on that past good experience, affirm with the poet that no doubt "the best is yet to be."

If we have offended you by the thesis of this book, by all means get on with your own life and marriage. Use the "manual" and the biblical foundations that seem best to work for you at this time. But if your marriage is "getting you down," we hope our story and our discussion of biblical images of marriage will give you new hope for turning an old marriage into a new one—at a yet higher and richer level. We salute you and leave you and your integrity to God's rich resources!

QUESTIONS PEOPLE ASK

Q: Do you mean to suggest that it is inevitable that young lovers will have to go through "all of the stages"? Why couldn't they start out as "whole person lovers"?

A: We believe they can. In fact, we think we have seen that phenomenon. Yet we suspect that the typical pattern will take a couple very quickly into the competitive, adversarial turf in their early marriage. How they move out of that battleground will be their personal journey. But the long years of maintenance often starve a marriage, if they settle down to a sort of legalistic co-existence. They really deserve to come back to mutuality and pleasure at a better level.

Notes

△

1. Young Love: Can This Be Eden?

1. All anecdotal names, except those used with surnames, are pseudonyms, out of respect for any possible embarrassment any part of any story might be. In most cases, anecdotes are "constructions" which pull together real past details from a series of similar events.

2. Co-Regency: "Let Them Have Dominion!"

1. See Ephesians 4:24 and Colossians 3:10 for St. Paul's three attributes of the image of God. The fabric of the "community responsibility" and ecological stewardship material is summarized and excerpted from Jurgen Moltmann, *God in Creation: A New Theology of Creation and the Spirit of God*, the Gifford Lectures, 1984–1985. San Francisco: Harper & Row, 1985. See Chapter VIII, "The Evolution of Creation," especially pages 186–191.

2. Genesis 1:26–31 and Hebrews 1:3.

3. See, for example, the discussion of these research bases in Donald M. Joy, ed., *Moral Development Foundations*, especially chapter one, "Life as Pilgrimage." Nashville: Abingdon, 1983.

4. Robert Coles and Geoffrey Stokes, *Sex and the American Teenager*. New York: Harper Colophon Books, 1985.

5. See Psalm 8.

6. Plaques, Inc., Box 1477, Carson City, Nevada, reprinted by special permission.

7. My colleagues who are immersed in the Old Testament tend to find themselves thoroughly embracing the "male Adam" perspective. They typically neglect to even interpret the Genesis 5 statement that

God created them male and female and called them Adam. Professor George Coats, for example, at Lexington Theological Seminary, in an unpublished paper entitled, "Strife and Broken Intimacy: Genesis 1–3: Prologomena to a Biblical Theology," describes Genesis 2: "The initial act of creation defines the moment with its focus on God's relationship with the man, the male." Coats goes on to describe the elegant position of the woman: "The word for 'woman' is a feminine form, *issah*, of the word for 'man,' *is* . . . . This act of naming is not the same as the man's act of naming the animals, [comparable, Coats says, to the 'naming' of Eve in Genesis 3] an act that symbolizes the man's dominion over the animals. Here, the name given the woman is the man's own name, an act that symbolizes a unique and intimate sharing of a common life. Neither party is lord over the other."

The bachelor male position is stated succinctly by Brevard Childs: ". . . the term *adam* is not used differently before and after the formation of the woman. Indeed, after her appearance *is* and *issah* are paralleled with *adam* and *issah* (vv. 23 and 25)." He goes on, ". . . the Masoretic tradition points the term man before the creation of the woman as a proper name, Adam, in 2.20: 'The man gave names to all the beasts, but for Adam there was not found a helper.' The Septuagint renders both occurrences of the noun in the verse as a proper name. In other words, according to both the Hebrew and Greek traditions the oscillation within the term is between *adam* as generic man, and Adam as one example of the species. It is not between a sexually undifferentiated earth creature and two examples of a sexually differentiated species. In ch. 2 *adam* who is representative man is instantiated in Adam." (See Brevard Childs, *Old Testament Theology in a Canonical Context.* Philadelphia: Fortress Press, 1985, pp. 190–191.) Childs, like so many other traditional, Western theologians and experts in the text, misses entirely the tragic "naming" of Eve which comes after the Fall and in the context of the consequences to the man by which the earth, all that grows from the earth, and the woman taken from his body are all reduced to "mere instruments" with only a functional value to him. Even the New International Version of the Bible erroneously uses a title, "Adam and Eve," within Genesis 2, but Eve is not the woman's name until after the Fall recorded in chapter 3.

8. See the opening paragraph of the Book of Hebrews (1:1–4), in any translation, to see how God "spoke" in the exact likeness of himself in his Son.

9. A. Cohen, *The Soncino Chumash.* London: Soncino Press, 1964, p. ix, 7.

10. We want to examine this issue in detail in Chapter 4. There we will cite further issues as well. See Jurgen Moltmann, *The Trinity and the Kingdom.* London: SCM Press, Limited, 1981. See especially his historical treatment of the capture of Christianity by the Roman Empire as a stroke of genius for making its theology over into a politically expedient model: monotheism to serve a monarchy, all vertical, with unquestioning obedience to those in superior positions in the hierarchy (Part V: A Criticism of Christian Monotheism, especially the section, "Monotheism and Monarchy").

11. Consider such a possibility put forward by Atuhiro Sibatani, "The Japanese Brain: The Differences Between East and West May Be the Difference Between Left and Right," in *Science/80*, December, 1980,

pp. 22 ff. Condensed from a Japanese language book, *The Japanese Brain: Brain Function and East-West Culture*, 1978.

12. For example, Ahuramazda, so one Middle Eastern legend goes, created a single human who, unfortunately, was killed. But its seed germinated in the soil and a plant grew up. When the flower appeared it had a stamen in the form of a woman and a man joined together. Ahuramazda plucked them, divided them, invested each with a soul, and released them to parent the human race. And Plato, the Greek philosopher, speaks authoritatively: "Our nature of old was not the same as now. It was then one man-woman, whose form and name were common both to the male and to the female. Then said Jupiter, 'I will divide them into two parts.'" Plato goes on to describe the two humans after the division: "When their nature had been bisected, each half beheld with longing its other self" (Plato, *Symposium*, Chapter XIV). The legend of a single human divided into two sexes is widespread. Most of the stories are fanciful, playful, even ridiculous. The idea of an Adam who was both male and female has been present in Jewish and Christian thought from ancient times.

13. C. S. Lewis, *Miracles*. New York: The Macmillan Company, 1947. See especially the chapter, "Miracles of the Old Creation," pp. 159 ff., and especially the footnote on "myth" embedded in the chapter, p. 161.

14. Donald M. Joy, *Effects of Value-Oriented Instruction in the Church and in the Home*. Bloomington: Indiana University dissertation, 1969, available from University Microfilm, Ann Arbor, Michigan.

15. Jo Durden-Smith, "Male and Female—Why?" *Quest/80*, October, 1980, pp. 15 ff.

16. Susan Muenchow, "The Truth about Sex Differences," *Parents*, February, 1980, pp. 55 ff.

17. In the paragraphs above, we have adapted a segment of an address, "Toward a Symbolic Revival: Creation Revisited," presidential address, October 26, 1984, at the Association of Professors and Researchers in Religious Education, assembled in Chicago. The address was published in *Religious Education*, Vol. 80, No. 3, Summer, 1985, pp. 399 ff. It appears also in a refined and later version, under the same title in *The Asbury Seminarian*, Winter, 1985, Vol. 40, No. 2, pp. 10–22.

18. See my extensive discussion on "sexual differentiation of the brain," with bibliography, in *Bonding: Relationships in the Image of God*. Waco: Word, Inc., 1985. See Chapter 5, with bibliography in notes on pp. 122 ff.

19. Karl Barth, *Church Dogmatics*. Vol III/1, p. 214, also III/4, pp. 116–240, tr. J. W. Edwards et al. Edinburgh: T. & T. Clark, 1958, p. 214.

20. See *Bonding: Relationships in the Image of God*, especially the chapter, "Parents and Children: For Each Other."

21. Exodus 25:12, 14; 26:27, 35; 27:7; 36:25, 31, 32; 37:3; 38:7; 2 Samuel 16:13; and Job 18:12.

22. See St. Paul's "Adam" references in Romans 5:1–2, 12–21, and also in 1 Corinthians 15:45–49.

23. We find the biological possibilities amazing, but are stopped short by the conclusion of Edward L. Kessel that Jesus was androgenous— carrying the morphology of a male, but the genetic code of a female—in his "A Proposed Biological Interpretation of the Virgin Birth" (*Journal of the American Scientific Affiliation*, pp. 129 ff., September, 1983). Paul

Jewett in his *Man as Male and Female: A Study in Sexual Relationships from a Theological Point of View*, Grand Rapids: Eerdmans, 1975, offers a parallel argument for an "androgenous" Jesus. While Kessel's biological speculations are impressive, our understanding of the incarnation of God in Jesus keeps us steady in accepting the genetic and morphological maleness of Jesus. His designation as "the son of God" seems gender specific and not at all ambiguous.

3. "He Shall Rule Over Her"

1. William M. Logan, for example, in his *In the Beginning God* (Richmond: John Knox Press, 1957), notes that "Interpretation of [the meaning of 'The tree of the knowledge of good and evil'] requires careful attention to the Hebrew concepts that are employed. 'Knowledge' must be understood in the Biblical rather than 'academic' or 'theoretical' knowledge." See pp. 34 ff.

2. For a discussion of the egocentrism of "shame" which renders it incapable of "repentance" until it can be transformed into "guilt," see "Naked and Unashamed," in *Re-Bonding: Preventing and Restoring Broken Relationships*. Waco: Word, Inc., 1986, especially pp. 37–38.

3. Consult the Hebrew text or an interlinear version.

4. See the discussion of the Fall in *Bonding: Relationships in the Image of God*. Waco: Word, Inc., 1985, pp. 21 ff., where each of the three "consequences" is explained and where Harold Myra's version of the serpent is described.

5. For fifteen years now our students have been reporting moral reasoning scores on Heinz dilemma protocols. There has been a consistent shock wave which runs through the room when graduate community women, student wives, and mothers consistently score at low to middle Level B, compared to larger numbers of male subjects who score higher in Level B, often with traces of Level C using Hugh Oliver's scoring manual on Lawrence Kohlberg's moral reasoning criteria. Carol Gilligan, noting the same pattern at the Harvard office of moral development, has now completed research and first theoretical constructions indicating that women may have been discriminated against in the test construction. She reports her concerns in the book, *In a Different Voice: Psychological Theory in Women's Development*. Cambridge: Harvard University Press, 1982. Beyond her evidence that women organize moral reasoning around issues of affect and people values, it remains likely, however, that women may suffer, in general, from (a) a lack of delegated responsibility for making significant choices, and, hence (b) tend to "arrest" at the "what will people think if they know?" stage, which is the bottom rung, Stage 3, of Level B.

4. Intimacy, Trinity, and Family

1. See Genesis 19:22, especially the footnote in the New International Version which reads, "Massoretic text, an ancient scribal tradition *but the Lord remained standing before Abraham.*"

2. See 1 Kings 19:11–13.

3. See Jurgen Moltmann, *The Trinity and the Kingdom: The Doctrine of God*. New York: Harper and Row, 1981, pp. 194–195. The

historical, philosophical, and theological components of this thesis are nicely developed in Moltmann, especially in Chapter six, "The Kingdom of Freedom," condensed particularly in the section, "Criticism of political and clerical monotheism," pp. 190 ff. Moltmann says that the Cappadocian Fathers and Orthodox theologians, to this day, stress "community." Not only do they focus on community, they criticize the modalistic tendencies in the "personal" trinitarian doctrine of the Western church (p. 199). Moltmann's presentation of the Caesars' reasoning explains how Christianity was chosen to serve the political agendas of the monarchy:

"The polytheism of the heathen is idolatry. The multiplicity of the nations which is bound up with polytheism, because polytheism is its justification is the reason for the continuing unrest in the world. Christian monotheism is in a position to overcome heathen polytheism. Belief in the one God brings peace, so to speak, in the diverse and competitive world of the gods. Consequently Christendom is the one universal religion of peace. In place of the many cults it puts belief in the one God. What political order corresponds to this faith in the one God and the organization of his worship by the one church? It is the Emperor Augustus's kingdom of peace, seen as Rome's enduring obligation and commitment, and as the common hope of the nations (p. 194–195)."

Moltmann's central point is that Christianity in the Western world was profoundly influenced by the conception of political power and the structure of the monarchy. This monarchial influence, he holds, has verticalized our conception of the Trinity, of all social order whether religious, political, or industrial. So "vertical" was the union between Christianity and the Roman and, later, other European emperors that absolute unilateral power was attributed to the emperors quite apart from whether they honored God either personally or by their arbitrary decisions. They were thus able to live in passive obedience to the vertical monarchy that governed their temporal lives, even to execution by the whim of a caesar or a king.

4. See also L. Hodgson, *The Doctrine of the Trinity.* New York: Charles Scribner's Sons, 1944, p. 95; cf. also A. M. Allchin, *Trinity and Incarnation in Anglican Tradition.* London: Oxford University Press, 1977; cf. also Geervarghese Mar Osthathios, *Theology of a Classless Society.* London, 1979, pp. 147 ff.

5. "Head of the House": God's Order for Families?

1. Donald M. Joy, *Effects of Value-Oriented Instruction in the Church and in the Home.* Bloomington: Indiana University dissertation, 1969, available from University Microfilm, Ann Arbor, Michigan.

2. We cited some of the clear evidence that women score higher on "feeling" and men on "thinking" on a standardized personality profile exam. For some of the clearer background data on the Myers-Briggs Personality Inventory and interpretative material, see the tabular and validation information in Isabel Briggs Myers, *Gifts Differing*, available from Consulting Psychologists Press, Inc., 577 College Avenue, Palo Alto, CA 94306.

3. Order the sermon version videotape from Discipleship Development Ministries, SPO 944, Wilmore, KY 40390 at $20. See the Word, Inc. list-

ing for the videotape series, *Relationships in the Image of God,* where the seminar version of "Creation, Adam, and Woman" is one of six titles.

6. "Chain of Command": The Naturalistic Fallacy Goes to Church!

1. Since 1971, we have carried out private research and writing from The Center for the Study of Children, Conscience, and the Family. *Catalyst* is a newsletter which reports on research well before it goes to a wider public, and is available quarterly. For information, write to SPO 944, Wilmore, Kentucky 40390.

2. Mark Wade, a student here in the Fall of 1984, took an off-the-cuff remark and drove it all the way through to construct a philosophical history of the naturalistic fallacy. Today Mark teaches at Friends Bible College in Haviland, Kansas. He reminded us again that our students surely have taught us more than we have taught them. We have summarized some of his findings here.

3. Clair Safran, "A New Redbook Survey: 65,000 Women Reveal How Religion Affects Health, Happiness, Sex and Politics," in *Redbook,* April, 1977, pp. 126 ff.

4. Shere Hite, *The Hite Report: A Nationwide Study of Female Sexuality.* New York: Dell Publishing, 1976. See also her *The Hite Report on Male Sexuality.* New York: Alfred A. Knopf, 1978.

5. Robert Coles and Geoffrey Stokes, *Sex and the American Teenager.* New York: Harper Colophon Books, 1985.

6. For a glimpse of "how we work," look at our discussion of the "three witnesses" in *Bonding: Relationships in the Image of God.* Waco: Word, Inc., 1985, pp. 35–37. We also do an illustrated presentation on the same topic in the opening videotape, *The Mystery of Human Bonding,* in the six-tape series, *Relationships in the Image of God.* For information on these and other instructional materials, write to Center for the Study of Children, Conscience, and the Family, 1985, SPO 944, Wilmore, Kentucky 40390.

7. On Silencing Women in the Church

1. Esther James, in "Our Foremothers: Julia Arnold Shelhamer," in *Daughters of Sarah,* March 1976, reprinted in *The Best of Daughters of Sarah,* November-December, 1981, Vol. 7, No. 5, pp. 10–11.

2. Glen Williamson, *Julia: Giantess in Controversy.* Winona Lake: Light and Life Press, 1969, pp. 15, 50.

3. See Chapter 6: "'Chain of Command': The Naturalistic Fallacy Goes to Church!" for a detailed review of the real basis for the effort to teach the curse as "gospel" in the church.

4. Joel 2:28–32.

5. It was Gilbert Bilezekian's seminal work, *Beyond Sex Roles: A Guide for the Study of Females in the Bible* (Grand Rapids: Baker, 1985) which magnificently put in perspective much of what we were struggling with in the New Testament epistles. Here and elsewhere in this chapter, we are particularly in his debt.

6. Berkeley Mickelson, "Women in the Church," a paper presented at the Baptist General Conference, Spring, 1980. See also Robert Rood

Moore, "Dilemma of Interpretation: Illustrated by Paul's View of the Role of Women in the Church." Unpublished paper at Asbury College, Wilmore, Kentucky, ca. 1982.

7. Gilbert Bilezekian, in *Beyond Sex Roles: A Guide for the Study of Female Roles in the Bible.* Grand Rapids: Baker, 1985, pp. 173–184. When we began to read through Dr. Bilezekian's book it was almost too much to take in. We grabbed our Bibles to check out his interpretation, and ended up reading his extensive footnotes right along with the basic text.

8. For further discussion of *authentein,* see Richard and Catherine Kroeger, "Ancient Heresies and a Strange Greek Verb," *Reformed Journal,* March, 1979, pp. 12–14, and their "May Women Teach?" *Reformed Journal,* October, 1980, p. 17.

9. See Bilezekian, pp. 144–156, especially the correlating footnotes and citations to other interpreters and interpretations of the text in 1 Corinthians 14:31–40.

10. Stephen Bedale, "The Meaning of Kephale in the Pauline Epistles," *Journal of Theological Studies,* n.s. 5, 1954, pp. 211–215.

11. Wayne Grudem, "Does *Kephale*" mean "Source" or "Authority over" in Greek Literature: A Survey of 2,336 Examples, in *Trinity Journal,* Vol. 6, No. 1., Spring 1985, pp. 38–59.

12. Fred D. Layman, "Male Headship in Paul's Thought," in *Wesleyan Theological Society Journal,* Vol. 15, No. 1, Spring, 1980, pp. 46–67.

13. Herman Ridderbos, *Paul: An Outline of His Theology.* Grand Rapids: William B. Eerdmans, 1975, pp. 380 ff.

8. Head and Body: The Complete Adam

1. "The Sacrament of the Last Supper" was created by Salvadore Dali at the suggestion of Chester Dale who suggested it in 1954 when Dale was the president of the National Gallery of Art. For those who would wish to probe the philosophical roots of the painting, it would be appropriate to consult Salvadore Dali's autobiography, titled *The Secret Life of Salvadore Dali* (New York: Dial Press, 1942). There he writes that by 1941, he was forsaking surrealism as bankrupt, along with the collectivist, atheist, and neo-pagan utopias, which he had studied in the writings of Karl Marx and Rosenberg, the Nazi. After studying theology, Dali began to believe that the spiritual forces for the reconstruction of Europe lay in "a reactualization of the Catholic, European, Mediterranean tradition . . . ." The painting, when we studied it in the mid-60s was hanging in Gallery 60-B, the Chester Dale Collection, of the National Gallery of Art, Washington, D.C., USA.

2. Continuing study on sex differences tends to pare away many cultural and "learned" differences. But the "bottom line" now includes not only the genital differentiation, with its compounding effects in bone development affecting height, muscle versus fatty tissue development affecting body build, but also brain development and utilization. Somewhere within this morass of complicated but subtle differences lies "affect," or feelings. Women tend to have a more consistent tendency to let "people dimensions" influence their judgments than do men, at a percent comparison of 60 to 40 when the two factors are placed on a continuous spectrum. For additional reading on this specific factor, con-

sult the statistical data reported in David Keirsey and Marilyn Bates, *Please Understand Me: Character and Temperament Types.* Prometheus Nemesis, Box 2082, Del Mar, CA 92014.

3. See Ken Druck, *The Secrets Men Keep.* Garden City, NY: Doubleday, 1985. In a *Chicago Tribune* interview with Dr. Druck he reported that he finds most men helplessly locked in a "fix-it" mode. They have difficulty listening with empathy to anyone, but tend to feel it is their obligation to rescue the tellers from the trouble they are reporting, usually with an outpouring of verbal advice.

4. See our original discussion of the purpose of human sexual differentiation in *Bonding: Relationships in the Image of God.* Waco: Word, Inc., 1985, especially pages 15–21.

9. Jesus Has a Plan for Families

1. We began this story at the opening of Chapter 5.

2. Matthew 20:25–28, New International Version. Compare also *Living Bible* for the "heathen . . . kings are tyrants . . ." language.

3. You will find the original published draft from which these lines were adapted in Kahlil Gibran, *The Prophet.* New York: Alfred A. Knopf, 1963. They are from the chapter on marriage, pp. 15–16.

4. Gilbert James, "The Use and Abuse of Power: A Study in Principalities and Powers," in *The Asbury Seminarian: The Wesleyan Message in the Life and Thought of Today,* Vol. 30, No. 1, October, 1975, pp. 6–23.

5. M. Scott Peck, *People of the Lie: The Hope for Healing Human Evil.* New York: Simon and Schuster, 1983, p. 129.

6. Peck, pp. 76–77.

7. See James W. Fowler, *Becoming Adult, Becoming Christian: Adult Development and Christian Faith.* San Francisco: Harper & Row, 1984, pp. 102–105.

10. "Head": Another Name for Husbands?

1. Paul Brand and Philip Yancey, *In His Image.* Grand Rapids: Zondervan, 1984. See chapter ten and eleven, "The Source," and "Confinement," pp. 120 ff.

2. Two wonderful books which deal with the importance of "blessing" in human relationships are Gary Smalley and John Trent, *The Blessing.* New York: Thomas Nelson, 1986, and Karl A. Olsson, *Come to the Party.* Waco: Word Books, 1972.

3. Basic body differences, including that of musculature, are explored in several popularly written articles on sex differences. These typically cite interviews with the primary researchers, with generous quotations. See, for example, Pamela Weintraub, "The Brain: His and Hers," in *Discover,* April, 1981, pp. 15 ff. See also Jo Durden-Smith's, "Male and Female—Why?" in *Quest/80,* October, 1980, pp. 55 ff.

4. Beyond the sex differences cited above, see also David Gelman, "Just How the Sexes Differ," *Newsweek,* May 18, 1981, pp. 172 ff. This and other reports focus on the "spatial" or mapping sense which seems to excel in males.

5. Diane McGuinness, in her amazing article, "How Schools Discriminate Against Boys," *Human Nature*, Vol. 2, No. 2, February, 1979, pp. 82–88, reports very different uses and skills related to vision, including likely connections between three-dimensional depth perception and higher mathematical operations.

11. "Body": Another Name for Wives?

1. See Paul Brand's description, with Philip Yancey, *In His Image.* Grand Rapids: Zondervan, 1984, p. 141.
2. See the section, "What a Head Needs Most" in Chapter 10, where we develop more fully some of the "body" gifts.
3. See *Bonding: Relationships in the Image of God.* Waco: Word, 1985, p. 102.
4. Compare Chapter 10, section, "Husbands as Heads," and its footnotes for additional information on brain differences.
5. See McGuinness, "How Schools Discriminate Against Boys," as well as Pamela Weintraub's "The Brain: His and Hers," both cited in previous chapters.

12. The New Adam: From Image to Likeness?

1. John Wesley, ed. Nehemiah Curnock, *The Journal of John Wesley, A. M.* London: Robert Culley, n.d., Vol. I, 465–467.
2. John Wesley, *The Letters of the Rev. John Wesley, A. M.*, ed. John Telford, Volume VIII. London: Epworth Press, 1931, p. 140.
3. Wesley, *Letters*, V, p. 16.

Subject Index

193

Scripture Index